IN SEARCH of an explanation for the strange occurrences that have filled her books, Adi-Kent Thomas Jeffrey traveled abroad to check the sources. She tracked down the mummy case of the High Priest-ess of Thebes, for example, whose curse, it is said, led to many deaths as the relic traveled from owner to owner. Mrs. Jeffrey found it in the British Museum, and, after much research, was able to refute one of the legends about it and to confirm the facts.

PARALLEL UNIVERSE contains this story, and some never-before-revealed su-pernatural experiences the author herself has had among the unusual phenomena she reports. It in an exciting chronicle of the "unexplained;" but, even more intri-guing than the tales themselves, is Mrs. Jeffrey's scientifically based theory that connects the origin of these events with a **PARALLEL UNIVERSE.**

Books by Adi-Kent Thomas Jeffrey

Parallel Universe
The Bermuda Triangle
They Dared The Devil's Triangle
Triangle of Terror and Other Eerie Areas

Published by
WARNER BOOKS

PARALLEL UNIVERSE

by

Adi-Kent Thomas Jeffrey

WARNER BOOKS

A Warner Communications Company

WARNER BOOKS EDITION

The author is grateful for permission to quote:
from *Grapevine*, edited by Morten Gale, Founder of the New Jersey Psychic Information Society.
from *Psychic* Magazine, 680 Beach Street, San Francisco, California 94109, passages from "UFOs: The Psychic Component" by Jacques Vallee, Ph. D. (*Psychic*, Vol. February 1974); passages from "ESP and The Universe and Man" by Milan Ryzl, Ph. D. (*Psychic*, Vol. February 1970); passages from "X Energy & Consciousness" by John White (*Psychic*, Vol. February 1976).
from *Supernature* by Lyall Watson. Copyright © 1973 by Lyall Watson. Used by permission of Doubleday & Company, Inc., and Hodder & Stoughton Limited.
from *Worlds-Antiworlds: Antimatter in Cosmology* by Hannes Alfven (W. H. Freeman and Company, 1966).
from *Black Holes: The End of the Universe* by John Taylor. Copyright © 1973 by John Taylor. Used by permission of Random House, Inc.
from STAR TREK LOG THREE by Alan Dean Foster. Copyright © 1975 by Paramount Pictures, Corp. Used by permission of Ballantine Books, a Division of Random House, Inc.
from STAR TREK LOG FOUR by Alan Dean Foster. Copyright © 1975 by Paramount Pictures, Corp. Used by permission of Ballantine Books, a Division of Random House, Inc.
from "Were These Children From Another World?" by John Macklin (*Grit*, December 1966). Used by permission of Grit Publishing Co., Publishers, and BP Singer Features.

ISBN 0-446-89305-6

Cover art by Sketch Pad Studios

Photograph section designed by Helen Roberts

Warner Books, Inc., 75 Rockefeller Plaza, New York, N.Y. 10019

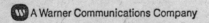 A Warner Communications Company

Printed in the United States of America

Not associated with Warner Press, Inc. of Anderson, Indiana

First Printing: June, 1977

10 9 8 7 6 5 4 3 2 1

Acknowledgments

My forever thanks to that untiring researcher and ferreter of facts, Bettie Metzner; and to Dolly Gish, typist-and-interpreter-of-scrawl beyond the best—both good and giving friends who contribute so largely to making my books possible.

To Ron, who always finds the best of both worlds

The mere formulation of a problem is far more essential than its solution, which may be merely a matter of mathematical or experimental skill. To raise new questions, new possibilities, to regard old problems from a new angle requires creative imagination and marks real advances in science.

ALBERT EINSTEIN

Contents

Introduction 13

Chapter One
    A Universe Beyond? 21

Chapter Two
    UFO's—Unidentified Fourth-Dimension
    Objects? 25

Chapter Three
    An Interdimensional "Door"? 39

Chapter Four
    The Solitary Vanishers 51

Chapter Five
    Clues from Crews? 65

Chapter Six
    The Philadelphia Experiment 79

Chapter Seven
    Is Time the Tunnel from Here to There? 91

Chapter Eight
    This Way to the Nearest Exit 99

Chapter Nine
    Where Did They Come From? 118

Chapter Ten
    Strange Forces 126

Chapter Eleven
    Pyramids and Tombs—Sources of
    Forces? 134

Chapter Twelve
    The Unseen Universe of Consciousness 170

Introduction

Man's place in the Universe has long been one of his most formidable puzzles. He feels he can no longer assume he is alone in this vastness of stars, suns, and encircling planets beyond count. There may be—and in all probability are—other forms of intelligent life. The present challenge is to locate and communicate with those "home planets."

Now, even more recently, a new possibility pops up for consideration: Not only may man not be alone in the Universe, but the Universe itself may not be alone in the mind-boggling system known as Creation. Is there another Universe like us existent, unknown to either man's eyes or his instruments? Does this invisible replica of us function "parallel" to us? Even around and within us, perhaps?

Do we have a Twin beyond the edge of Space and outside of Time?

No one knows the answer yet, but the question is startling, daring and surprisingly old. It was first presented in 1799 by a French nobleman, astronomer and mathematician named Pierre Simon, Marquis de Laplace. Laplace did painstaking research on the motions of heavenly bodies. He published his theories in his work, *Mécanique Celeste*. He stated that a sufficiently massive star that collapsed in old age would become invisible because the escape velocity from the star's surface would be faster than light and therefore, since no light could escape its surface, it would be invisible (referred to today as a "Black Hole").

A little over a hundred years later, a German genius named Karl Swarzschild contributed further and more meaningful conclusions about the collapsed star. He determined that the ancient contracting star which has spent all its fuel and is imploding produces such enormous gravitational pull as it collapses that a certain point of "no return" for any approaching object is set up. This point is established when the star has shrunk to a size so small it is only one billionth of its former radius. This critical state of a collapsed star, inside of which all objects are trapped forever, is called, after its discoverer, the "Swarzschild Radius."

In his recent book, *Black Holes: The End of the*

Universe?, author John G. Taylor presents the Swarzschild Black Hole concept (and Professor Taylor should know well that of which he writes, as he is presently Professor of Mathematics at Kings College, University of London, prior to which he held chairs of physics at the University of Southampton and at Rutgers University in New Jersey).

Taylor discusses the Swarzschild theory in relation to the possible existence of twin Universes. The Swarzschild solution "can be visualized best for flatlanders, a land inhabited by people," asserts Taylor, "so thin that they have height and width but no thickness. The world would be truly flat, very distant from the centre of the Swarzschild Black Hole, but as the flatlanders approached nearer to it it would be as if the land was sliding down the edge of a funnel, getting smaller and smaller, and more and more curved. The double funnel obtained by joining another funnel to the first at their ends now completes the picture. A flatlander's journey to the centre of his universe would continue with his passing through the most curved part, the 'throat' of this double funnel, and so out into an ever flatter landscape just like the one he was originally in."

A few paragraphs later, Taylor reports on this theory with: "Here is a puzzle indeed, the duplication of a single universe by the power exerted by gravity . . ." Then he concludes almost sadly, as if with a sigh, that such twin Universes have never been seen, nor can we expect them to be, "since to cross from one world to the other across the throat without being crushed to death by intense gravitational fields at the centre can only be achieved by travelling faster than light. The superiority of the speed of light to all other material things is one thing which is sacrosanct even inside the black hole, so we may never know about the other universe joined so pathetically to ours, if it is described, as it could be, by the Swarzschild solution."

Philosophers are not bound by "sacrosanct" postulates. Lobsang Rampa is one such learned man. A Tibetan lama, this noted mystic maintains that there exists a world of antimatter exactly like our known world of matter. Everyone and every object on Earth, he feels, has a counterpart of the opposite polarity in another galaxy in another system of time altogether. This dual existence, asserts Rampa, has effects, one upon the other, when a "slit" in one world comes into juxtaposition with a "slit" in the other. The "slits" become "avenues of interrelation," it can be said. Almost all of Earth's inexplicable phenomena that have been occurring for centuries are the result of such an interrelationship coming into play during juxtaposition.

The concept of antimatter exists in scientific as well as philosophic thought. In his book, *Worlds—Antiworlds*, Hannes Alfven (Professor of Plasma Physics at the Royal Institute of Technology in Stockholm, Sweden) presents findings and theories that he finds necessary to comment on with:

"The foregoing may sound like so much science fiction, Nothing of the kind . . ."

What did the "foregoing" consist of? Discussing the discovery of elementary particles and their natural symmetry—that is, a *proton* was found to be complemented by an *antiproton*. Then Alfven goes on to say:

"When the antiproton was discovered, it aroused not so much surprise as satisfaction. The symmetry of elementary particles was now an experimental fact. Both the electron and proton had antiparticles, twin brothers in every detail except for the electric charge. Nature, in short, did not distinguish between positive and negative electricity!"

A few paragraphs farther on, Professor Alfven invites our awe with the statement, "Should an object of antimatter be brought into contact with ordinary matter, it would act like a bomb . . . The result would be just as violent if an object of ordinary matter were introduced into the world of antimatter . . ."

Shades of science fiction, indeed!

Psychologists, as well as philosophers, have gotten on the "Other Universe" bandwagon. Parapsychologist Stanley Krippner sees such a possibility as the result of further insight into the psychic world of man's mind. In an interview with Paul Chance for *Psychology Today* magazine (October 1973) Dr. Krippner (who is President of the Association for Humanistic Psychology and is associated with the Dream Laboratory of the Maimonides Medical Center in New York City) stated that many physicists all over the world are beginning to talk about particles of matter that are unstable in time and space—scientific thinking which brings up the possibility that there are different Time Universes with which we could interact.

World-renowned physicist, chemist, and parapsychology researcher, Milan Ryzl, has devoted years to the study of cosmological theories. Educated at the University of Prague in Czechoslovakia, Dr. Ryzl came to this country in 1967 and has been actively engaged in the study of man and his Universe ever since. In an interview with *Psychic* magazine (January 1970), Dr. Ryzl commented on cosmological theories of ESP.

"These theories presuppose that the Universe of astronomers, which appears to be composed of matter dispersed in a three-dimensional space and changing in a one-dimensional time, is, in fact, only a minor part of a far more extensive reality that comprises additional dimensions inaccessible to sensory perception ... Nor is it beyond comprehension, then, that the super-Universe contains beings or civilizations other than those of our immediate knowledge ..."

Here you might ask: How is it possible for man to be surrounded by, comprised within, and even affected by a dimension or Universe completely inaccessible to any of his sensory perceptions?

My good friend, a scientist and philosopher, Morten Gale (founder of the Psychic Information

Exchange of Riverton, New Jersey), can give you an illustration.

The frog, he once noted in a newsletter to his society (June 1976), sits on a lily pad in the middle of his pond looking very much the master of his domain. The observer watching the frog may think the little jumper is seeing the same pond the onlooker sees. But not so. The frog's eye responds only to sharp boundaries, convex curves that move, and changing contrasts in illumination, such as when a large shadow passes over him.

The physical structure of the frog's eye allows only for the detection of what the creature needs for food, such as bugs of small curvature, or to defend itself from predators by jumping out of large moving shadows.

In much the same way, continues Gale, other creatures of our world live in the same physical globe as we do, yet they are, at the same time, not in our world at all, as far as their senses go. Bees, bats, moths, dolphins and countless other species live out their lives in various corners of our world, sensing and responding to those energies and forces important to their survival and completely unaware of those beyond their ken or need.

In such a way, hints Gale, so may man.

"Our physical Universe may be just one part of a larger 'Multiverse,'" concludes Gale.

Dr. Milan Ryzl would agree but would surely add the statement he made to his *Psychic* magazine interviewer:

"All of these ideas, though, remain nothing

more than fantastic possibilities unless they are confirmed by compelling scientific evidence."

Where and in what form will such evidence likely emerge?

In this book we will take a look at fascinating incidents of phenomena wherein, many researchers feel, lie the basic clues.

Chapter One

A UNIVERSE BEYOND?

A spaceship hurtled through space. The light beyond the windows of the craft was blindingly violet. The two men staring into the lavender void felt their muscles tense with apprehension. Where were they headed? What awaited them?

They began to exchange ideas.

" 'There may be two centers to our galaxy. A spatial one from which all can be measured—and another on which certain different forces converge.'

" 'That is it, Captain . . . and it is that second convergence of forces that we appear to be traveling through to its end—'

"A violet light seemed to be blending, running together into a smooth maroon pool. They struck it seconds later . . .

"As the *Enterprise* moved through it, nonspace began to coalesce, to take on a single form. It gradually became a kind of circular tunnel . . .

"They existed in a cylindrical universe . . .

"Spock looked up. 'I am afraid that our normal navigational references mean very little here, Captain. All readings indicate that we are not in time as we know it . . . we are no longer in space as we know it . . .' "

Some time later Captain Kirk turned to his companion and asked, " 'Are we in an alternate universe?' "

Blood-stirring science fiction of the highest order, the above passages are quoted from *Star Trek*. Spock's and Kirk's exploits got sensational fan ratings when they appeared in story form in the popular paperback series, STAR TREK, Logs One, Two, Three and Four by Alan Dean Foster (based on TV scripts).

But, as is so often the case with sci-fi, the wild fiction may be but a shadow of the form yet to be seen. Might there *be* cylindrical entrances to other universes? Might there *be*, as Star Trek has depicted it for years, a positive and a negative universe in existence—parallel Universes?

If this is so, and we here in our provincial Universe have, indeed, an invisible counterpart that interrelates with us from time to time (as more and more theorists are coming to believe), what and where is it?

Plato had an answer over two thousand years ago. In his work, *The Republic*, this Greek philosopher expounds his theory that this Universe in which man lives is but a shadow of the real Universe. To illustrate his point he depicts men chained in a dark cave, their faces to the wall, their backs to the opening of the cavern. They see shadows on the wall of men and events and believe they are seeing reality. So blinded are they by this illusion that should one man escape his bonds, turn and see what is really going past the cave's aperture, and eagerly tell his companions about it, they would not believe him. They would scoff and scourge him—spit on him and even kill him, concludes Plato.

Is man still so reluctant to learn what is the truth about himself and his world? No, it seems he is ready to look beyond what he is seeing.

For example, not so long ago a piece appeared in the papers stating that scientists at the Bartol Foundation in Swarthmore, Pennsylvania, had developed a method that could aid in proving a long-existing theory: that there may be entire galaxies in our universe that are made up of antimatter—invisible duplicates of the galaxies we know. If there can be invisible galaxies, it seems only one more cosmic step to conceive of invisible universes. As mentioned in this book's introduction, more and more scientific theories are supporting such a claim.

And so, we may have a duplicate "out there" that is closer than we dare to imagine. Let us move on from that thought to a point beyond imagining and let us start thinking—constructively—about any and all clues that may be hinting such a possibility.

Chapter Two

UFO'S—UNIDENTIFIED FOURTH-DIMENSION OBJECTS?

Should "UFO's" be considered an abbreviated term, not for "Unidentified Flying Objects," but for "Unidentified Fourth-dimension Objects?" Are UFO's challenging clues to an alternate universe?

Astrophysicists the world over are trying to stretch man's knowledge to determine just exactly what UFO's really are and where they come from. No scientist is listening or striving harder than Dr. Carl Sagan, head of the Astronomy Department at Cornell University and an ardent researcher into mysteries of our cosmos. Dr. Sagan organized the first scientific symposium on flying saucers in the

1960's. He is still active in writing, listening, and researching in the field.

Tackling the puzzle with a scientist's usual pragmatism, Dr. Sagan wrote for the opening page of his book, *Other Worlds*, "I cannot say that I believe there is life out there. But it is possible. Some of us think it is probable. Our first halting steps into space have shown us other worlds far stranger and more interesting than imagined by authors of the most exotic fiction."

But in approaching an examination of these possibilities of outer-space visitors to earth, Dr. Sagan displays his skepticism in illuminating fashion. "Just from logical considerations," he says over and over, "it is as unreasonable to expect aliens to visit earth as often as claimed as to expect an elf called Santa Claus to service millions of homes within an interval of eight hours on Christmas Eve."

In another book of his, *The Cosmic Connection*, Dr. Sagan presents the astronomical approach to the possibility of aliens visiting earth from outer space. Employing reasonable astronomical assumptions to estimate the number of advanced civilizations that might exist in our galaxy, Dr. Sagan determines that each of them would have to launch 10,000 missions a year to account for even one annual visit to earth! And Sagan's colleague, the noted physicist, Hong-Yee Chiu, makes a related point: he calculates that the total mass of metals involved in all of the space visitation reported in the history of our planet (basing the

UFO size roughly on the shape and mass of our Apollo capsule) would require that the total mass of half a million stars be processed and all their metals extracted! Or, taking the point to a finer analysis and assuming that only the outer several hundred miles, say, of stars like our sun can be mined by advanced technologies (as farther in, it would be too hot), one finds that two billion stars must be processed, or approximately one percent of all the stars in our galaxy!

Neither possibility, one is forced to admit, sounds very likely.

For such reasons, other renowned scientists such as the world-famous astronomer, Dr. J. Allen Hynek, present their general agreement that the idea of actual "nuts and bolts" craft coming from outer space is a very naive interpretation.

Allen Hynek, chairman of the Department of Astronomy at Northwestern University, expressed his views on the UFO phenomenon to the publisher of *Fate* magazine, Curtis Fuller, in the June 1976 issue.

Dr. Hynek is a distinguished scientist and professor, having served as Director for NASA's Optical Satellite Tracking Program from 1956 to 1960, a service which gave him charge of the establishment and operation of twelve tracking observatories around the globe. Dr. Hynek has also served as scientific consultant to the Air Force on the UFO puzzle from 1948 until a few years ago when he established the Center for UFO Studies, an organization which collects reports of UFO sightings and sends out newsletters and reports.

Mr. Fuller asked a direct and provocative question: "You once suggested to me that UFO's might be three-dimensional projections from elsewhere."

"[Such an idea] would explain so many things," answered Dr. Hynek. "One characteristic of the UFO phenomenon is that it is highly isolated in both space and time. It's here, and then it's gone."

Later on in the interview, the scientist expanded on his theory that the UFO solution may lie farther out than outer space—that some unknown intelligence seems to lie behind flying saucers. "Whence [comes] this intelligence?" he asks. "Is it a product of our own minds without our being aware of it? Is it from a parallel Universe?"

Dr. Hynek is first to agree that scientists don't have the answer. "It's a research problem. In research you don't know all the answers."

A well-known scientist in Italy has been spending many years of his life striving to come up with a possible solution to the UFO enigma. In a recent article for the *Journal of Centro Richerche Biopsichiche* published in Padova, Italy, Professor Guiseppe Bonfante came up with the same possible answer as that of Dr. Hynek.

"There may be parallel Universes," he declared. UFO's may be from "a galactic civilization" which has reached a stage of technological know-how far in advance of ours, perhaps millions of years beyond ours and is now "exploiting a form of energy unknown to us." This energy, proposes Bonfante, enables these intelligences to produce "a force field which modifies the fundamental constants of matter of any object by means of which the same object suddenly disappears from the visible universe, entering another dimension beyond time and space."

So to the serious researcher into UFOlogy, it is becoming increasingly clear that he must look elsewhere for a source of the "flying saucer" than simply outer space.

Where, then?

A distinguished French astrophysicist, Dr. Jacques Vallée, offers the same answer as do his colleagues in America and Italy. Dr. Vallée is probably the most dedicated scientific UFO researcher in the world, having written over twenty learned articles in British, French and American journals, as well as three books in English about the UFO phenomenon.

This scientist's conclusions were concisely stated in an interview he gave *Psychic* magazine in January 1974:

"The things we call 'Unidentified Flying Objects' are neither objects nor flying. They can dematerialize, as some recent photographs show, and they violate the laws of motion as we know them . . .

"The current tendency to accept UFO reports as 'evidence' of visits from space travelers is a nonsequitur. The phenomenon could be a manifestation of an advanced technology in a much more complex sense, involving, for example, interpenetrating universes."

A picture accompanying this interview shows clearly a saucer-shaped object rising from the ground in successive stages, as each stage materialized, then dematerialized.

Once again we are led to consider this newest and most revolutionary theory: parallel Universes. On close examination, it seems UFO's don't *come* from other planets or galaxies or *go* to anywhere. They just *appear* and *disappear* as though arriving and vanishing through some interdimensional "door."

Thousands upon thousands of UFO spotters have testified to such seemingly impossible comings and goings of inexplicable objects in the sky.

My husband and I are two such witnesses.

One summer evening in 1948 we were sitting out on our back patio gazing at a serene stretch of nighttime sky when a startling thing caught our attention.

Over the distant treetops, but near the edge of the horizon, five bright lights were suddenly visible. They moved silently along in a smoothly progressing line, one after the other. My husband commented that the objects were moving too slowly to be airplanes.

After a few seconds, the leading light suddenly flicked upwards at a 90° angle. Then the second, third, fourth, and fifth followed in quick succession. As each did so, it changed from a white glow to an orange-red. Then the procession continued as before. In the next moment, they vanished—just like that—one, two, three, four, five, and gone from sight! They didn't fade away. They just disappeared as though, one by one, they had gone through some invisible "door" in the sky!

This "here-one-minute-and-gone-the-next" class of sighting is typical of thousands that have been recounted over the twenty-eight years since that summer evening. The objects witnessed and their characteristics seem almost identical. None are more arresting than the following incident that occurred ten years after my sighting.

It was the night of October 3, 1958. Train #91 of the Monon Railroad was headed south from Monon, Indiana, to Indianapolis, a distance of about ninety miles.

The train's five crew members were all experienced railroad men. Three of them, Harry Eckman, engineer, Cecil Bridge, the fireman, and Morris Ott, the brakeman, were all in the cab at the head of the train. The conductor, Ed Robinson, and the flagman, Paul Sosby, were in the caboose at the rear of the train. The two groups were in touch with each other through FM radio.

Shortly after three in the morning on October 3rd, the train crackled through the village of Wasco. Peering ahead in the darkness, Engineer Bridge noticed four peculiar lights in the sky ahead. Although starlike in appearance, it soon became clear the objects were not stars. They were lights moving in a kind of V formation.

Bridge called out to the other two men in the cab. The fireman and brakeman stared out into the night, their eyes wide with amazement. Four big soft white lights were moving in a procession across the tracks about a quarter of a mile up ahead. The men estimated the lights were traveling at about forty-five to fifty miles an hour as they glided over.

Then, abruptly, they stopped and came right back!

This time they were zipping along and in no time at all had shot out toward the east and disappeared—still at very low altitude, scarcely clearing the treetops of the countryside.

In less than a minute, they reappeared and were now coming along the line of track headed straight for the oncoming train!

Quickly, Bridge radioed to the men at the rear.

Conductor Robinson leaped into the cupola where he could see over the top of the fifty-six freight cars they were pulling.

He was astonished to see four "blobs of light" hovering over the diesel engine, only as far from him as the length of the train! They were coming steadily on toward the caboose. In seconds, the flagman, Sosby had scrambled up into the cupola with him. The two men didn't say a word but watched in awe as the four lights swung over them headed north as they were facing south, gliding in the opposite direction above them no higher than a few hundred feet over the train. Moving no faster than about fifty miles an hour, the men estimated, the procession of lights proceeded agonizingly and terrifyingly slowly.

As the weird formation pulled away from the caboose, the two men stared hard. The objects were four large disk-shaped "vehicles" about forty feet in diameter. They each glowed with a kind of phosphorescence, their edges "fuzzy" and indefinable.

The two men rushed out onto the rear platform and gaped at a strange spectacle. The four lights continued beyond the train about half a mile; then they paused, assembling into a "bunch" about a mile away at this point.

In the next instant the four lights pulled out into a line of procession, one right behind the other, and glided eastward. As they moved away they seemed to pick up in speed. The faster they traveled, the brighter they got. At this point, all five crew members of the train were witnessing the weird phenomenon. As the lights pulled away, the men all observed the same thing: the objects glowed and dimmed in sequence; first, number One; then Two; then Three, and finally Four. At the same time, the objects changed color from bright glowing white to an orange-yellow.

But this was not the end of the fantastic incident.

A few minutes later, the procession of fuzzy lights appeared again, coming right down the length of tracks behind the freight cars and overtaking the train at a fast clip. Two of them, the men at the rear noticed, were flying "on edge."

Robinson ran quickly into the caboose and

seized a flashlight. It was a powerful five-cell, sealed-beam model that could throw a beam a good distance. The conductor switched the flashlight on and directed the rays right on the moving saucers.

The moment the beam hit them, the objects jumped sideways out of the path of light. When the formation of disks swung around and started following the train again, Robinson flashed his beam at them once more. This time, as if in consternation, the group of objects scattered. From that time on, the glowing saucers did not fly close over the train any more. They "hung around" beside the train and behind it, keeping a good distance away until the freight train rumbled into the town of Kirklin, some thirty-eight miles northwest of Indianapolis. There the strange formation pulled away to the northeast and in seconds had vanished from sight.

This remarkable incident was written up in the Monon Railroad's employees' magazine later on that year and was also covered by the late famed television news commentator, Frank Edwards, on his Indianapolis news show. Edwards also used the incident in his book, *Flying Saucers: Serious Business*. Very few saucer-sightings have incorporated such a lengthy period of observation. The case will remain a classic in UFOlogy files.

But there have been many other accounts of strange, round, and vanishing saucers. Listen to this report from a former U. S. airman, Francis O.

Sullivan, a retired Air Force master sergeant who now resides in Tucson, Arizona. Sullivan (known to his buddies as "Sully") served for eighteen years of the twenty-eight he was in the Air Force as a radar operator at air bases both in this country and in Japan.

One of his most memorable experiences occurred at an Air Force Base near Masawa, Japan, in 1951. The former master sergeant described the incident in a recent interview with the *National Enquirer* (April 20, 1976).

"An officer pilot named Brigham was in the air and I was in radio contact with him when he sighted something and went after it. He radioed, 'I've never seen such a thing! It's round . . . I don't know what it is . . . when I started closing in on it, it must have—it's gone, Sully, it's gone! Just gone!' "

In the late 1960's, a writer-cartoonist, Otto O. Binder, ran a syndicated picture-panel feature in newspapers all over the U. S. He entitled his presentation *Our Space Age*. Readers from far and wide were avid followers of the feature and contributed many of their personal experiences to the creator. Mr. Binder discussed these accounts in an article he wrote for *Fate* magazine in Febraury 1968. He put an accent on those experiences which he labeled "oddball" because, unlike sightings of disks, cigars, and opalescent globes, this "vanishing breed" mangled any of the current theories, such as interstellar travel.

Bruce Maroot of Wayne, New Jersey, wrote Mr. Binder:

"I am an amateur astronomer and I am very interested in UFO sightings. . . . Last September, 1965, I happened to gaze westward at the setting sun. All of a sudden, a silvery oval object streaked across the western sky. It vanished as suddenly as it came. Suddenly another shot across the sky and that disappeared in the same spot as the first. . . ."

Bonita Rodgers of Walnutport, Pennsylvania, contributed this experience:

"I went swimming August 23rd (1966) with my cousin. When we were walking down the towpath, it suddenly appeared in broad daylight. It was long and silver . . . then it disappeared into thin air."

John Gucci of Penquannock, New Jersey, wrote Mr. Binder of a similar experience:

"In July, 1965, my friends and I were . . . outside at night and saw two giant red circles go slowly across the sky. . . . When they reached a certain spot, they disappeared."

One of the most interesting accounts received by the author-cartoonist came from Sara Huff of Ann Arbor, Michigan, in 1966. Ms. Huff told of seeing that previous May a "silvery thing" in the sky.

"I could not tell the size because the sun was reflecting off of it. Now I have seen a weather balloon and I know what they look like. They move slowly and don't disappear. I have also seen a satellite and they move slowly across the sky and don't disappear. But mine disappeared, just like that, leaving no sign whatsoever of its being there! It disappeared right before my eyes. I searched the skies but I couldn't find anything."

Such accounts stirred a question in the thinking of Otto Binder: Why do so many UFOs seem to materialize out of thin air and vanish just as inexplicably?

Binder received his answer in a letter from Dr. Jacques Vallée:

"Consider all the well-documented sightings of objects which appear or disappear *suddenly* or change shape. Also the Type II phenomena (mother ships) with the materialization of the craft inside a luminous cloud . . . We should pay special attention to such cases. They may give us a breakthrough in physics. Everything seems to work as if these observers (of UFO's) had been successive projections into our three-dimensional space of objects of a higher dimensionality. This is not incompatible with the idea of either space travel or time travel, but it adds a new element—the indication that by a study of UFO reports considerable insight could be gained into the nature of our environment, perhaps leading to a revision of our notions of space and time."

Author Binder incorporates the most titillating question of all time after assessing all the experiences and concepts contributed to him:

"Do UFO's visit earth through 'interdimensional holes?' "

We will look at evidence that may point to the

existence of an invisible "doorway" through which people and objects come and go, passing from one dimension to another.

Chapter Three

AN INTERDIMENSIONAL
"DOOR"?

In a recent TV movie success, *Beyond the Bermuda Triangle*, the hero (Fred MacMurray) loses his sweetheart (Hope Lange) in another inexplicable vanishing in this area of strange disappearances (a subject I covered in my book, *The Bermuda Triangle*). The hero makes a final desperate move at the end of the story in an effort to find the missing girl. He readies his yacht for a trip out into the mysterious Bermuda waters, then tells his friends of his purpose.

"Somewhere out in that area there's a door—and I'm going to find it!"

A few days later his boat is found. It is deserted.

No one is aboard. The viewer realizes that the man succeeded in finding that "door" and went through it, as had so many others before him. The audience is left with the strange comfort that the hero and his fiancée are united in some other dimension.

The story was a popular one. Yet it was hardly believable. Or could it be? Could, in fact, there exist some invisible doorway to a Universe beyond our present knowledge?

If such an alternate Universe could exist—and we have examined the many theories propounding that it very well might—then would it not be equally feasible—even logically likely—that there is an interconnecting "link" between these two parallel worlds?

Let us take a look at what might constitute evidence of such an opening.

People have been mysteriously vanishing from the face of the earth for centuries—and perhaps they have been travelers through an interdimensional hole as we will investigate in a subsequent chapter in this book—but for the present let us take a look at those remarkable instances in which people and/or objects *literally* dropped from sight! In other words, they disappeared when they were in full view of witnesses. They simply ceased to be where they were an instant before!

For example, take the incredible incident that once took place on a Vermont bus going from South Albans direct nonstop to Bennington. James E. Tetford, a resident of Bennington, had been visiting relatives in South Albans. After his visit was over, he boarded a bus for his hometown. He was seen getting on. The conductor collected his fare, just as he did with the other occupants of the vehicle. Sometime later, the bus pulled into Bennington. The driver called out the stop. The passenger who had boarded at South Albans and bought a ticket for Bennington was not getting off. The driver called out the stop again and turned around. The man who had asked for Bennington was not on board!

The driver testified later and several fellow passengers stated that the man named James E. Tetford had gotten on at South Albans but *had not gotten off the bus at any time en route!* How could it be that he was not on board when the bus pulled into Bennington? He could not have jumped off a moving bus or been thrown out without the driver or any of the other passengers seeing him. How could a man just evaporate?

No one knows. But such inexplicable vanishings have occurred and may be rare cases of interdimensional traveling.

The most famous case of complete obliteration happened on September 23, 1880, on a horse-breeding farm about twelve miles outside of the little town of Gallatin, Tennessee, close to Nashville.

The farm was owned by David Lang, who lived there with his wife and two children, eight-year-old George and eleven-year-old Sarah. David's prize show horses grazed in a pasture in front of the house and were a familiar sight to neighbors driving past.

On this particular September morning David stepped out onto his front porch with his usual vigorous stride and halted a moment to talk to his two children who were playing with a new toy— a wooden wagon pulled by two wooden horses. Mrs. Lang stood behind him smiling at the momentary family "togetherness" before the day's chores for each of them.

In the next instant, her husband waved a lean hand and with one bound was down the porch steps and gone quickly into the field, headed toward the barn.

Mrs. Lang shielded her eyes from the morning sun as she gazed after her husband for a long moment. Suddenly her attention was caught by a carriage creaking up the long farm lane. She swung her gaze over to catch sight of a buggy driving up the roadway in a tiny cloud of dust.

How long this past dry spell had been, she thought to herself as she began to make out the forms of the vehicle's occupants. It was her brother. With him was the town's most respected legal mind, Judge August Peck.

Oh, she decided, she would ring the big bell and call David back. He would surely want to talk to their visitors. She was sure he did not see or hear them coming.

She lifted one hand to ring the bell as she looked out at the swift striding form of her husband, now in the middle of the large pasture. Before she could finish the movement, her eyes blinked in utter astonishment. The walking figure she was gazing at suddenly vanished! In mid-pasture, without any change of stride or turn of the head or warning of any kind, the man was gone from sight!

At that identical moment, Judge Peck, in the buggy, stopped his conversation with Mrs. Lang's brother and turned toward the field where he spotted David Lang. He started to call out to him. He wanted to talk to David. The judge had opened his mouth to shout when his jaws dropped wide open in amazement instead. Lang vanished in thin air!

"My God," stammered Austin Peck, "what happened to him?"

"What are you talking about?" asked his companion.

The judge squirmed in his seat, both irked and disturbed.

"I tell you, I was just looking at Lang crossing his field when he suddenly disappeared. Let's get out there and find out what happened to him."

The two men climbed out of the buggy and strode quickly across the field. Mrs. Lang had already started out, running to the spot where her husband had last been seen.

The group met in speechless consternation at the spot.

"He must have fallen into a hole somewhere," suggested the judge.

"But it was so sudden, and he didn't seem to sink

away or slip out of sight—he simply vanished," cried out Mrs. Lang, nearly hysterical at this point.

There wasn't a sign of a disturbance or crack or hole of any kind in the flat grassy stretch of field. They searched every inch with care.

Finally the three ran back to the house. The brother rang the big bell as hard as he could, summoning all and any help that could come. Soon dozens of neighbors, friends, and townspeople arrived. Every corner and square foot of land was searched for a possible crack or hole. Absolutely nothing was found in a field completely barren of trees, bushes, stones, or anything but grass.

As hours stretched into days and days into weeks, not a clue was forthcoming. Mrs. Lang and her brother summoned a surveyor and a geologist who examined the field and found only that there was a bedrock of limestone several feet underground. But there was no fracture anywhere in this bedrock. Not so much as a small crack, much less a cavernous hole.

Still not satisfied, neighbors banded together and bored holes searching for possible underground openings or sinkholes. There was not a sign of such a thing. Not even the grass where Lang had been walking looked disturbed. There simply was not a single clue turned up that could give a solution to what happened to David Lang in the middle of his pasture one sunny September morning in 1880.

There has not been a solution to emerge in the near hundred years since the incident.

A year after the strange occurrence, something happened to set everybody in Gallatin talking about the case once again. It was noticed that the famous spot whereon David had vanished was strangely marked by nature. Within a circle area of some ten feet in diameter, the grass had grown tall and thick. Not a single animal on the farm would graze there. It was also free of insects. Nothing seemed to want to go near that circle. Except David Lang's two children.

Young George and Sarah went into that lush green circle to play frequently. From time to time, Sarah would call out,

"Father, are you anywhere around?"

One day in early August of 1881, Sarah called out to her father as was her custom and suddenly a voice responded. Both she and her little brother heard it. It was a distant cry for help. The children ran back to the house and told their mother. Mrs. Lang hurried out to the spot as fast as she could. She called out just as the children had done. She heard an answer from her husband! It was unquestionably his voice!

For several days, subsequent to that morning, the three went out to the circle and called out to David Lang. His answering voice was heard by all three of them, but each day this occurred, they noticed the reply was coming through fainter and fainter. Finally by the fifth day, there was no answer at all. It was never heard again.

The strange experience of a person vanishing within sight of a witness was repeated within a decade of the Lang incident. It involved no less-respected a citizen of the world than a member of the distinguished British publishing family of Macmillan, founders of one of the largest publishing firms in the world.

It was on July 13, 1889, that one of the adventurous Macmillans was visiting legendary Mount Olympus in Greece. With him was a friend by the name of Hardinge. There was also a local guide. The three men started out on horseback and rode until they reached a plateau at the base of two peaks. Hardinge decided to tackle the highest peak; Macmillan elected to climb the lower one. The guide remained at the base below the two peaks to hold the horses. He was within easy calling distance of both men.

Hardinge reached the summit of his peak and turned to look down on his friend, who had already attained the summit of the lower peak. The two friends waved. With that, Macmillan turned on his heel and started downward. Hardinge stayed awhile gazing at the beauty around him, then looked for his friend again below. He spotted Macmillan about halfway down his slope. Then in the next instant there was nobody there! Hardinge stared in disbelief. The slope as far as his eye could trace to the bottom was empty, without a sign of a soul. What had happened to the man?

Hardinge scurried down and at the base met the guide, who was also transfixed with amazement, staring intently at the slope of the lower peak.

What could have happened to him? The guide said he was watching Macmillan descend at the same time Hardinge happened to be looking at him. Both men had seen the Englishman there on the slope descending one moment, and then he was gone in the next!

The two men climbed to the exact spot where the gentle climber had last been seen. There wasn't a sign of him, his clothing, or his presence, nor was there any clue as to what could have happened to him. They searched every inch of the mountain area. Later, a search party joined in the quest for clues. Not a thing was found. Neither could any holes, cracks, or crevasses into which he could have fallen be unearthed. He had simply dropped from sight—vanished into thin air—as the other two were watching!

The master writer and researcher of all things strange and mysterious, Charles Fort, devoted his entire life to collecting data on unexplained phenomena. Fort uncovered an incident of disappearance in plain sight, strikingly similar to that of David Lang from his pastureland. Fort's case involved a farmer named Isaac Martin. Martin was working in his field within view of some members of his family, and he, just like Lang, dematerialized right where he was working in full sight of his family. That was on April 23, 1885—just five years after the vanishing of Lang.

As Charles Fort himself might have asked, "Is somebody collecting farmers?"

Or children? In August of 1869 in beautiful

County Cork in Ireland, thirteen children all vanished without trace, recorded Fort.

But the "interdimensional door" is not always used for people. It serves, it seems, as an entrance and exit for objects, too.

Take, for example, flying rocks. Rocks or stones have been witnessed for centuries flying or bolting at people or places right out of nowhere! (Several instances of this were covered in my book, *Triangle of Terror and Other Eerie Areas*).

This inexplicable and extraordinary phenomenon of flying objects fascinated the late Ivan Sanderson, Scottish-born geologist, zoologist, and science editor. In an article he wrote for *Fate* magazine (September 1963), Mr. Sanderson called for serious investigation by the scientists of the world into flying rocks.

He early made clear the details of what he was talking about. "The first thing to establish," he wrote, "is that the phenomena of which we speak appear to be but one of a class. All of these involve the appearance of objects at a location where they previously were not, and without discernible, known, physical (meteorological, mechanical, human, etc.) force being involved. Such objects can 1) just appear, 2) float in, 3) be lobbed or dropped, 4) be fired or projected. Curiously, it appears they never arrive in the normal manner, at the velocity expected if they had been truly thrown or dropped—meaning they never arrive at the speed prescribed by known gravitational pull, i.e. at a velocity of 32 feet per sec."

Later, after stating that such stones, when in motion, are not obeying the known, proved Newtonian laws of physics, Sanderson asks, "What laws, then, *are* they obeying?"

He never gives us an answer. He begs for research that can ultimately supply one. He does give us an intriguing instance in which he himself experienced the puzzle of flying stones.

"I was sitting on the verandah of an estate house in Sumatra in the year 1928 with my host and hostess. . . . Suddenly, a small, shiny, black pebble came sailing in from the outer darkness. It rolled to a gentle stop by the back wall. I was not alarmed, but, admittedly, I was somewhat surprised. Then another stone came in, then another, and another. I now was alarmed and asked who was throwing stones at us.

"My host began cautiously. He said that such stones came in all night, almost every night, but that none had ever hit anybody. There was a moment of profound silence, though the party included half a dozen people, all 'outsiders' like myself.

"Then everybody wanted to know the cause of this. Why did our host tolerate people throwing stones at him night after night? Had he no control over his staff and his estate workers? Meantime, more stones arrived, bounced and rolled to a stop by the back wall.

"Our host invited us to pick up some of the stones and mark them with chalk (which he provided) . . . and then toss them as far as we could into the surrounding garden. This garden was extensive, with sweeping lawns, shrubbery and beyond, acres of tropical growth . . . so thick you could not force your way through it. We threw the small stones, duly marked, far out into this peripheral tangle. We must have thrown over a dozen such marked stones.

"Within a minute they were all back!

"Nobody, with a powerful flashlight or super-eyesight, could have found those little stones in that tangled mess, in that length of time, and thrown them back on the verandah. Yet they came back . . . !"

Toward the conclusion of the article, Sanderson presents his thoughts as he discusses where they might be coming from or going to. "Another space-time continuum; another Universe?"

It is a question we are beginning to hear over and over.

Chapter Four

THE SOLITARY VANISHERS

Not all the people who have "checked out" swiftly and mysteriously from this earth have done so in sight of others. They have vanished when they were completely alone. The most familiar prelude to such disappearances has usually been a last word to someone they knew that they were "going out for a while and would be back before long." Or words to that effect, clearly indicating their intention of returning.

No more baffling such experience has ever occurred than that of Dorothy Arnold in December of 1910. Her complete obliteration is a classic in mysterious disappearances.

The Arnold family at the turn of the century in New York City was one of the most respected, wealthy, and elite clans in the city's social register. Mr. Francis R. Arnold was the millionaire head of a perfumery and cosmetic firm. Dorothy was the second of four children in the Arnold family.

As December 1910 dawned, Mrs. Arnold was busy getting festivities arranged for the forthcoming debut of her eighteen-year-old younger daughter, Marjorie. Dorothy, twenty-five, having just returned from a visit with a former Bryn Mawr classmate living in Washington, D.C., pitched in to help with the preparations.

On December 8th, Dorothy finished writing the invitations for the coming-out party scheduled for the 16th and mailed them off. The next day, the young girl went to the bank, withdrew the modest sum of $36, went shopping along Fifth Avenue, and ended up at an art exhibit at the Metropolitan Museum.

On the 10th, Dorothy met a girlfriend for lunch. She was Elsie Henry, daughter of a Wall Street broker. After the matinee of a current popular show, *The Garden of Allah*, the two girls went to the Waldorf-Astoria for tea (at 34th and Fifth Avenue, at that time).

They made a date to meet for lunch on the subsequent Monday but on Sunday, the 11th, Dorothy called Elsie and cancelled the date, explaining that she had to go shopping for a dress to wear to her sister's party. "That will probably take me the whole day, but I'll call you later on in the week."

On Monday morning, December 12th, about eleven, Dorothy stopped by her mother's bedroom. The girl was dressed in a chic wool coat and a satin-trimmed velvet hat, and carried a black fox muff.

"I'm going shopping, Mama. I intend to find a dress for the dance if it takes me all day. I'm sure I shall be able to if I put my mind to it!"

Mrs. Arnold looked up from her dressing table. "If you'll wait a few minutes until I can get dressed, I'll go with you."

Dorothy waved off the idea. "Oh, no, Mama, don't bother. You have too much to attend to. If I find anything I like, I'll phone you and you can come see it."

"All right, dear," Mrs. Arnold smiled and watched her daughter tuck her two hands in her muff and pull away from sight down the thick-rugged hallway. In a few moments, she heard the front door slam shut. It was the last sight and sound she ever had of her daughter.

Others reported seeing her subsequent to that. A candy counter clerk at Park & Tilford's on the corner of Fifth Avenue and 57th Street remembered seeing the familiar customer come in and buy a half-pound box of candy about noon that day. A little before 2 p.m. she was seen coming out of Brentano's bookstore at 27th and Fifth by a friend, Gladys King, who was walking north on the avenue. The two nearly bumped head-on.

Both girls laughed and expressed delight at seeing each other.

"I'm just on my way to the Waldorf to meet Mother for lunch," said Miss King. "I'm fifteen minutes late already, but just a minute, I want to take time to give you this." She searched in her bag and pulled out a white envelope. "I received your invitation to Marjorie's party the other day, and here's my acceptance. I was just going to mail it, but you might as well take it along with you."

Dorothy laughed, thrust the letter into her black fox muff, and the two parted.

It was at that precise spot that Dorothy Arnold vanished from all human sight or ken. As the New York *Daily News* put it later, "She seemed to disappear as abruptly as a figure in trick photography!"

That night when the girl failed to arrive home for dinner, the Arnolds called all their friends with no success and finally summoned the family lawyer, a Mr. Keith.

The lawyer went over Dorothy's bedroom and all her personal effects with care. There was no indication that the girl did not expect to return. Her clothes were all in the closet, still hanging in their usual place. There was no sign of any kind of disturbance among the girl's personal belongings in her desk or dressers. The lawyer did find some letters from a gentleman friend of Dorothy's, a George S. Griscom, Jr., whose uncle was Lloyd C. Griscom, former ambassador to Italy. It turned out that George was in Italy at that time. The Arnolds cabled him asking if he had any information about their daughter. He replied, "Know absolutely nothing." A few weeks later, young Griscom hired a detective to join the search already going on by the Pinkerton Agency, hired by Mr. Arnold. But not a single clue was forthcoming. After four months of fruitless efforts, which included dragging the lakes in Central Park, the Arnolds called off the hunt, stating reluctantly that they had decided that Dorothy must be dead.

Nothing has been uncovered in the more than half a century that has followed to prove anything one way or another. Dorothy Arnold stepped into the fame of oblivion on that December morning. Nothing is likely ever to change that.

Thirty-three years later, New York City saw another mysterious disappearance of a beautiful young heiress. Her name was Valsa Anna Matthai, daughter of John Matthai, wealthy head of the Tata Chemical Company of Bombay, India. In the spring of 1944, Valsa was studying at Columbia University. She was staying at the International House near the university. She was last seen in the early morning hours of March 20th by the elevator operator at the House, a dormitory for foreign students.

"She rang for the elevator about a quarter to five," the man told the police later. "I took her down, noticing that she carried no handbag and was dressed very lightly for such a bad night." (At that moment a blinding snowstorm was in progress.) "She wore a polo coat with slacks, regular shoes, and only a flowered cotton kerchief over her head. She said nothing. She stepped out the front door into the white whirling snow, and that was the last I saw of her. She did not return."

The police found her purse in her room with money and her cosmetics in it. Her substantial account at the nearby Chase National Bank was untouched. Without any apparent reason and with no preparation the young heiress walked out of the International House and, like Dorothy Arnold before her, stepped into oblivion. There was never a trace of the young woman found, although the search was extensive, including a house-to-house search within a mile radius, the sifting of coal bins, the draining of water tanks, the dragging of the Hudson River, and the distribution of fifteen thousand circulars offering large rewards. Nothing ever surfaced to give one bit of information as to what had happened to her. It has not to this day.

If India mourned the loss of a beautiful young girl that year, it would not be alone in the Far East to suffer a mysterious vanishing. Thailand joined her nearly a quarter of a century later.

In March of 1967 James H. W. Thompson, Thai silk tycoon, who lived on the River Klong in Bangkok, Thailand, packed up for a few days' vacation and took off for what is known as the Cameron Highlands. His servants in his "House on the Klong" were so convinced that their master would be back no matter how long a time elapsed that they continued to keep his bedsheets changed and his dining room table set for nearly a decade after his mysterious disappearance.

But the fact remains that the millionaire who

steered the Thai Silk Company into world renown did not return, and it is a pretty safe assumption that he never will. What occurred on that vacation alone no one has any idea. Was he murdered? Did he get lost in the jungle? Was he accidentally caught in an animal trap? Eaten by a tiger? Kidnapped by the Communists?

Dozens of such questions have been asked over the intervening years, but not a single solid answer has come to the open.

"After such a long time, we assume he is dead," stated Jim's sister, Mrs. Thomas Reath of Flourtown, Pennsylvania, in an interview in 1970. Business associates in Bangkok still find it hard to accept that decree.

"Jim could not have been killed or abducted. There would have to have been some evidence left," commented a Thai businessman, Yindee Changtrakul, not so long ago. "As time passes, the mystery deepens. How is it possible for a man to evaporate?"

The wife of Andrew Carnegie Whitfield must have asked that same question a thousand times back in New York City in 1938. (Surely, Charles Fort would have asked at this point, "Is somebody collecting millionaires?")

Her husband, twenty-eight-year-old Andrew Whitfield, was a sixth-generation Whitfield and a nephew of Andrew Carnegie. In April of 1938 he had been Sales Manager for International Business Machines in Bethlehem, Pennsylvania. On the morning of April 15, in their New York East side apartment, young Andrew hurried through breakfast, reminding his wife that he was scheduled to leave the apartment at 9:30 in order to get an early start for Bethlehem. He was going to look over the city and seek out a suitable home to rent, as they would have to move to that Pennsylvania town in the near future. It was a step young Whitfield looked forward to with zest.

As they ate, Andrew told Betty that he had ordered his plane readied after winter storage. He chatted betweeen bites of toast. Betty nodded, not taking time to answer. She knew Andrew was always eager and hurrried to get behind the controls of his gleaming new monoplane, a Taylor Cub job with the name, *The Butch,* paintd on its cowl.

"Did you get the plane overhauled at Roosevelt Field?" asked Betty.

"Yep, had Weitz and Eveland of P.O.S. (Plane Owners Service) check it over."

Whitfield bolted down a last swallow of coffee and pushed back his chair, getting quickly to his feet. "I'm off now, dear. Be back tomorrow!"

With those words, Andrew Whitfield dashed out of the front door, and that was the last his young bride of ten months ever saw of him.

Betty waited all the next day, but there was no sign of her husband. She finally called her brother-in-law, John, who, in turn, started a minute-by-minute investigation. He checked out Roosevelt Field and found that Andrew had arrived there at about ten in the morning of the previous day. He had called a friend, Johann Frederic Johanns, Jr., on Long Island and had asked him to meet him at Brentwood Airport, twenty miles away. Johanns was there at the appointed time, some fifteen minutes later, but no silver monoplane ever came in.

Checking with Roosevelt Field, John Whitfield found that his brother had dashed into the airport in his car, then taken off in a flurry in his plane headed into the eastern sky. That was the last ever seen of the young millionaire.

The family alerted the Nassau Aerial Police, who scoured the open country between Roosevelt and Brentwood searching for wreckage. There was nothing. Searching parties tramped over woodlands and swamps. Nothing. Was it possible Andy had flown or been blown off course into the Great South Bay or the Atlantic Ocean or Long Island Sound?

"Hardly," said those who knew him. "He was too good a pilot. Also, the weather was clear and the wind was mild."

Was it possible Whitfield flew out to sea and committed suicide? "Oh, no!" exclaimed his brother. "Andy was too happy-go-lucky, too pleased with his job. He had too many plans for the future."

Flying friends crisscrossed all of Long Island by air. The Jones Beach Air Patrol and members of the Bureau of Air Commerce searched the local water areas for signs of the missing plane.

But there was no wreckage found—and no Andrew Carnegie Whitfield. From that day to this, no one knows what happened to the carefree, zestful young man with the big future ahead. Was his future to be lived out in another dimension? Did the silver monoplane rip through a "hole" into an alternate Universe?

One more inexplicable vanishing from the known into the unknown.

No mysterious disappearance will ever out-puzzle the famous case of Judge Crater.

In 1930 Justice Joseph Force Crater, genial forty-one-year-old Justice of the Supreme Court of New York, was one of the best-known figures in New York City. Supported by the powers of Tammany Hall, Crater was on secure footing politically. Experienced as a lawyer and a college professor, he was a man whose opinions were widely respected.

That summer of 1930, Crater and his wife, Stella, vacationed in their cottage at Belgrade Lakes, Maine. On the evening of August 3, a telephone call came in for the judge. Mrs. Crater described later how her husband had taken the call, then after hanging up announced he had to make a quick trip to New York City on business but would be back the following Saturday, the 9th.

Accordingly, the judge packed up and left Belgrade Lakes early the next day. On the morning of August 4th, he was at his five-room apartment at 40 Fifth Avenue. The Crater maid, Almeda Christian, testified later that the judge spoke to her that day, asking her to clean up the place on the 7th, Thursday, but not to come thereafter until August 25th, when he and Mrs. Crater would be home after the summer vacation's end.

At 1 p.m. on the day of the 4th, Crater was seen lunching at a restaurant on lower Broadway near Chambers Street. Between 4 and 5 p.m. he was seen in front of 130 West 11th Street where the judge made a call on Dr. Augistís Raggi.

The next day, Crater was seen in the corridor of the County Courthouse near his chambers, in the forenoon hours. He lunched that day with Justice Alfred Frankenthaler. That night he dined at Dr. Raggi's house, leaving there about half past midnight.

On August 6th, Justice Crater was seen at the courthouse by his secretary, Frederick Johnson. Later in the morning he went to his bank, the Chase National, and withdrew more than five thousand dollars in cash. Crater put the money in two business-size envelopes in the inside pocket of his coat.

Back in his chambers, the jurist borrowed a briefcase from his secretary and gathered together six manila folders. Into the case and the envelopes he stuffed a large batch of papers. Then Crater told Johnson to lock up the chambers. He announced that he would be back on the morrow.

At about 7:30 that evening, Crater stopped at the Arrow Theatre Ticket Agency and arranged for a seat for that night's performance of the Shubert musical, *Dancing Partners*. Then, a few minutes later, the justice entered Billy Haas's restaurant at 332 West 4th Street, a few doors away from the agency.

There Crater saw an old friend, William Klein, an attorney, sitting at a table with a showgirl named Sally Lou Ritz. Klein, who did legal work for the Shuberts, invited Crater to join them for dinner, which he did.

Meanwhile the ticket agency ordered a ticket held at the box office for Crater. It was picked up, but at what time and by whom was never discovered. Crater remained at the restaurant until 9:15, long past curtain time. It was at that point, according to the testimony of both Klein and Miss Ritz, that Crater parted from them outside the restaurant and climbed into a cab. The taxi moved off in a westerly direction.

That was the last authenticated glimpse anyone had of Joseph Force Crater, alive or dead.

What he did with the briefcase, the folders, or the five thousand in cash was never determined. (Although they mysteriously appeared in his bedroom dresser months later! They had not been there earlier when the apartment had been completely searched by the police.)

Crater's vanishing was relatively unnoticed, however, for several weeks, as Mrs. Crater did not report her husband missing until August 25th, when the couple were to leave Maine and return to New York. The office assumed he was in Maine, and Mrs. Crater assumed he was in New York. Where the judge actually went, no one—from that day to this—has ever been able to learn. He completely disappeared without a clue as to his where-abouts. In an article written in the July 25, 1950, issue, *Collier's* magazine dubbed the Crater case the "most tantalizing disappearance of our time."

But the prize for mysterious vanishing should definitely go to that Master of Mystery himself, the renowned 19th-century teller of terrifying tales, Ambrose Bierce.

Born in the Northwest Territory of Ohio in 1841, Ambrose Gwinnett Bierce grew up in a struggling home with two parents whom he later referred to as "unwashed savages." His youth saw him pro-gress from working as a handyman in a brick yard to becoming at age sixteen an outstanding reporter on a Chicago newspaper. He later fought in the Civil War with the Union forces and was dis-charged at the end of the conflict as a lieutenant. He eventually ended up in England in the years from 1872 to 1877 working as a journalist, and there he earned an excellent reputation as a writer. In later years, he returned to California and went to work in Oakland for William Randolph Hearst, writing a weekly column for the San Francisco *Examiner*.

Bierce's later life was as much a personal tur-moil as had been his youth. He was divorced from his wife and saw his two sons die under tragic cir-cumstances—one shot in a brawl over a girl, the other killed by excessive drinking. By the year 1909, Bierce was a melancholy loner, living in Washington, D.C., writing books and articles and, from time to time, traveling about the United States.

Late in 1913 Ambrose Bierce told friends and reporters he was going on another trip, probably to Mexico. He warned everybody that he would not be returning. He took off, leaving no forwarding address. Shortly before Christmas he wrote his daughter and several friends from Mexico. He told his daughter, Helen, that he had left a trunk with his manuscript biography in a hotel in Laredo, Texas. No such trunk or any such papers were ever located.

No trace of Ambrose Bierce was ever found after those letters of Christmastime, 1913. Dozens of interested parties tried to uncover information. Friends, relatives, journalists, the U. S. State and War Departments, and even Pinkerton detectives searched for any possible clue. Not one ever came to light.

Was the author shot by revolutionary forces? Did he suffer amnesia? Did he go berserk and disappear in anonymity?

Or did he, like many a solo exiter, somehow walk through a doorway from this dimension into another one, more real than any of those supernatural fantasies that his writer's mind had conjured up?

Not one of these famous "solitary vanishers" over the years, from Dorothy Arnold to Ambrose Bierce, has ever returned to tell us the answer.

Chapter Five

CLUES FROM CREWS?

If there is some hint of interdimensional inter-action to be deducted from the sudden obliteration of an individual (either when alone or while in a crowd), what can be the significance of a swift and unaccountable wiping out of a *group* of people—all simultaneously? Surely even greater meaning lies in such cases.

Strange and inexplicable as it may be that a person can be in a certain place one moment and utterly gone the next, it is even more incomprehensible that *several* individuals can all vanish at once without any apparent rhyme or reason and without leaving a single piece of evidence as to what happened!

Are there special clues to be found in crews vanishing?

If so, the many cases of "ghost ships" should be studied, instances in which vessels have been found afloat at sea perfectly intact and equipped, but entirely empty of their crews. All signs usually have pointed to sudden abandonment for no apparent reason. I covered several such instances in my book, *The Bermuda Triangle*, including mention of the famous *Marie Celeste* found deserted off the Azores in 1872 and the discovery of the abandoned *Carroll A. Deering* off Cape Hatteras in 1921.

Stories of these and other ghost ships have filled volumes of literary investigation. One such tale is the following experience told and retold since it happened on February 28, 1855.

The sailing ship, the *Marothon*, was cutting through the winter-tossed waters of the mid-Atlantic when its captain spied another vessel, close by, heaving and falling in the churning sea.

The master of the *Marothon* studied the ship through his glass. Its name was the *James Chester*. He swept his spyglass the length of the vessel. He saw her rigging was tangled and her decks were in a state of disorder. The master hailed the ghostly ship, but there was no answer. Finally, a boat was lowered and the silent ship was boarded by sailors from the *Marothon*. The men searched the vessel from bow to stern. There was not a living soul on

board. Although there was wild disarray everywhere, there was no sign of violence. There wasn't
a trace of blood found, or any signs of a struggle,
or any kind of weapon picked up. The ship's
papers were missing, and her compass, but
strangely, *every lifeboat was in its place!*

The search by the *Marothon* discovered that
there was no lack of provisions, and water was
abundant in supply. The ship itself was as sound as
if it had just been launched. Yet there remained
not a single piece of evidence to explain why an
entire crew would abandon a ship in the middle of
a wind-whipped ocean!

In 1850 at Easton's Beach near Newport, Rhode
Island, residents saw a strange vessel heading in
for shore, all her sails set and her flags a-flutter in
the offshore wind. Minutes later she beached,
serene as a queen. It turned out that the ship was
the *Seabird*. She was under the command of Captain John Huxham. She was due in to Newport
that day, after a voyage to the Honduras.

Men climbed on board the stranded vessel with
unabated curiosity. They found coffee still hot on
the galley stove, a warm breakfast laid out on the
table for a hungry crew, and all the charts and
navigational instruments intact. But the only creature still on board was a small dog, sitting on deck
as though awaiting rescue with calm assurance.

Thorough investigation into the abandoned *Seabird* followed the ghostly discovery at Easton's
Beach that day, but not a single conclusive clue
was turned up. What made a whole crew desert

a perfectly sound ship in fair weather? Where did they go? And why?

That dimensional "door" again, perhaps?

Crews have not only vanished from ships but from aircraft as well. Sometimes with the airplane, sometimes without it. For example, a strange incident occurred in the Iraqi desert of Mesopotamia in July of 1924. Two British Air Force pilots (Flight Lieutenant W. T. Day and Pilot Officer D. R. Stuart) crashed in the sandy stretches and were given up by their fellow officers after a length of time with no sight of the returning men. But eventually a search party came upon the craft. It was perfectly intact and still had petrol. What astonished them was the discovery of the footsteps of the two men imprinted in the sand as they distinctly, side by side, marked a progressive path from the plane into the desert some forty yards away. Then abruptly the footsteps stopped. There was nothing else there. No rock; no vegetation; no sign of any animal tracks. Not a thing. There was no indication of a scuffle. No trace of any other presence—human or animal. No dead bodies or parts of any bodies. The desert swept outwards from where the footsteps halted without a vestige of anything being visible. It seemed, the would-be rescuers said later, as though the two pilots had been "sucked up into the air!"

The U. S. Air Force scratched its collective head thirty years ago over the vanishing of a treasure-laden transport plane on December 4, 1945. The craft, carrying seventeen persons, took off from its home field near Monrovia, Liberia, and headed for Accra in British West Africa. It was a routine flight covering seven hundred miles off the Gold Coast. The plane carried a cargo of an undisclosed amount of gold and silver. Twelve hours later, when the huge transport had still not touched down at Accra, an investigation was launched. Search parties by air and by sea took in 112,500 square miles. They couldn't turn up so much as a burned matchstick or a uniform button from any of the crew.

For six months, the Air Force pursued the strange case. Finally, in June of 1946, the U. S. Army stamped "Unsolved" on the file of the vanished treasure transport over Africa. It is still regarded as one of the Air Force's biggest mysteries.

The crew included the pilot, Lieutenant Oliver K. Morton of Wichita, Kansas; Corporal Samuel Mehrman of Linden, New Jersey; Corporal Samuel K. Klink of Irvington, New Jersey; and Sergeant Seymore J. Stanger of New York. Did these men and their companions hurtle through some invisible "door" into another dimension—plane and all?

Then there are the fantastic cases of whole troops vanishing while in open sight (documented by the late Frank Edwards, news commentator, author and researcher of phenomena). A contingent of six hundred and fifty soldiers of the French Colonial Troops stationed in Indochina set out on a march across open country in the year 1858. They tramped briskly off on a countryside road headed for Saigon about fifteen miles away. They never arrived. Nor was the smallest trace of any of the men, their equipment, or their bodies ever found. The entire contingent dissolved on a march through wide-open country!

Equally baffling is the incident that took place in 1939 near Nanking, China. Some three thousand Chinese soldiers were stationed on the outskirts of Nanking to prevent any attack from hard-pushing forces of the Japanese infiltrating that area. A short time later, the outpost troop did not respond to radio contact from within the city, Puzzled, a Chinese Army colonel at Nanking sent out an aide to investigate. When the military aide got to the spot where the roadblock had been set up, he found the entire outpost of troops gone. Their guns had been placed in neat stacks beside low-burning cooking fires, but there wasn't a sign of a human being in the area! Three thousand soldiers could not have all deserted simultaneously—and made their way successfully across open country without being detected!

Yet, three thousand men vanished without a trace!

Take, also, the mystery of what happened in *midair* to two experienced flyers in a Navy blimp, the L-8, in 1942. The L-8 took off from the Navy base at Treasure Island with every moment of flight watched by the crews of two patrol boats. When the blimp finally returned to earth, it was empty! Neither man had been witnessed falling out of the blimp into the sea, yet it had been under constant observation! What could have happened to two men in steady view from below who were surrounded by nothing but air?

What could have happened to a three-man crew of a lighthouse in the Outer Hebrides off the west coast of Scotland in 1900?

The Flannan Islands are a group of seven small isles off the west coast of Lewis, one of the larger and better known islands of the Outer Hebrides (as forlorn and wild a group as I ever saw!). The Flannan group's history goes back to ancient times. Always too rocky and wild for habitation, they were used in olden days for burial rituals of the dead. There are the ruins of an ancient chapel still to be found on one of these isles, the largest of the Flannan group, called Eilean Mor. Like its six brothers, the rocky peak is simply the tip of a mountain buried in the sea. There is scarcely any vegetation, nor even the sight of a bird nest, so barren and bleak is it rising in gaunt silhouette against the cold Atlantic ocean and sky.

But lying close to the traffic of the Scottish and Scandinavian shipping lanes, the Flannan rocks have always presented a menace to ships. Wrecks of countless vessels stacked up on the rocky shores over the centuries. Finally in 1899 the British government decided to build a lighthouse on Eilean Mor. It was stoutly built—some seventy-five feet high—on top of a rocky projection over two hundred feet above the sea. Its huge searchlight "eye" —a light of 140,000 candlepower—was designed to be visible for twenty-five miles out in the ocean in good weather. As a landing spot for the lighthouse, steps were carved out of the rock above each of two docks on the west and east sides, affording two possible accesses to the place and giving a choice in the event of heavy winds or tides. In late December of that year of 1899 a crew of four men reported for duty at the lighthouse. The schedule was fair and workable for such an isolated duty: every two weeks a ship from Lewis would arrive with mail and supplies and leave with one man aboad to take a vacation on the mainland, leaving his three fellow sailors on duty at the lighthouse. In this way, each man got two weeks on shore and six weeks on the island. For a year all went smoothly. Then came the winter of 1900.

On the 6th of that December, the supply tender, *Hesperus*, operated by the Northern Lighthouse Board, arrived and took aboard the man next in line for vacation. He was Joseph Moore, a husky Scottish former seaman who picked his way down the icy steps now with fervor. "Aye, what a welcome sight to weary eyes and heart ye be," his heart sang as he climbed onto the tender. He looked back at the gaunt lighthouse standing like a tight-lipped sentinel against the blasting sea winds.

He squinted his eyes but, of course, there was no spotting the remaining lighthouse crew. Only the gray gaze of the "eye" in the tower. But in his mind's vision he knew the lonely pain each man was feeling as he looked out over the empty expanse of ocean bearing away the only sign of life they'd be seeing for another several weeks. He felt for each of them—Tom Marshall, Don McArthur, and most especially, Jim Ducat, who had just returned from his leave. Two glorious weeks of mainland were behind him now and would not come again for another month and a half. So was the fate of each of the crew—each in his turn.

But for now, Moore did not allow himself any further such melancholies. He wanted only to anticipate and savor the luxury of his forthcoming freedom.

The two weeks that followed were superior to any Moore had ever seen in those parts for December. He felt unusually blessed. There had been virtually no storms, and the weather had been what one might call almost docile. The sea, he'd noticed also, was remarkably calm. The happy weather made his return to the lighthouse post even harder to contemplate. But return he must. On December 21st, Joseph Moore boarded the *Hesperus*. Soon after leaving port, almost as a reprimand to the duty that required the Scot to go back into cold limbo, the area burst out into as wild a storm as ever Moore had seen. The tender made no effort to progress. It decided to ride out the storm hugging the Scottish coast as close as it dared for protection.

On the third day the *Hesperus* made a try for Eilean Mor. But the sea was so violent there was no chance to attempt a landing. For two more days, the tender marked time out in the water within sight of the unyielding lighthouse tower.

But as the crew of the tender stared, something strange was obvious to them all.

"Odd," commented the captain, "but there hasn't been a light comin' from that tower in the past two nights! 'Ave ye noticed, Moore?"

"Aye, 'tis strange it is, Cap'n, for not one of the three men would be derelict of his duty to tend that light. I can't understand it. Aye, indeed I cannot. Mayhap something be wrong?"

By the morning of the 26th, the sea was as calm as it had been earlier in the month—smooth as blue-green glass. The tender chugged in toward the east landing, her signal flag fluttering in the morning wind. Soon the shrill blast from her whistle cut through the air. But contrary to the usual, there was no answer from the lighthouse. No responding signal flag. No sight of any of the three keepers scurrying down the steep stone steps, eager for the mail and news from the mainland.

Baffled, the captain ordered a succession of blasts from the tender's whistle. Nothing in return. Not a sound or sight of a soul.

Uneasily, Joseph Moore shifted the weight of his bag from one shoulder to the other and prepared to climb off the *Hesperus*.

"Wait, Moore. We'll be comin' with you. Something be wrong, certain sure!" With that, the captain bolted over the side with the other man. About a half-dozen sailors from the tender joined them.

As the group neared the top of the steps, close to the base of the tower, Moore looked upward and called loudly, "Ahoy! Marshall! McArthur! Ducat! Where be ye?"

Only the wind answered in an icy wail.

Moore turned and stared at the captain.

"Somethin' be wrong, Cap'n. Let's hurry"

The men bolted up the remaining stairs, threw back the lighthouse door, and plunged into the inside. Everything in the living quarters was in order. But the clock had stopped and the fire in the stove gone out. The air was cold as a tomb.

Moore dashed up the stairs to the light, his heart missing a beat with every step. Something had happened, but he couldn't figure out what. Something awful. He just knew it.

He examined the giant glass "eye." The wicks had been cleaned, properly and thoroughly, and trimmed. The lens had been polished. But he noticed the cloth that was usually put over the light in the daytime was not in place.

At that point, Moore remembered the log the keepers always kept. He found it. The last sentence was written on December 15th by Tom Marshall. It stated simply, "God is over all."

Moore's head shot up in surprise. He'd never heard Marshall or any of the other two men ever talk about God.

He pored over the earlier entries, starting with the day he had left for the mainland. The sentences were plain and standard, recording the time and the weather. But one thing was odd. The entries mentioned a storm. There had been no storm reported in those environs during the past two weeks! Not until the one just passed that had delayed the tender. But that could not have been the foul weather referred to during the 12th and 13th. What storm were they talking about?

Then there was the surprising comment on the very day that Ducat had just returned from vacation. He was recorded by Marshall as being "irritable." Why, Moore asked himself, would a man just returned from a holiday be in a bad mood?

Even more startling was an entry on the following page stating, "Ducat quiet. McArthur crying."

"Crying!" Moore shook his head in disbelief. A big hunk of seaman who'd weathered the worst gales sent by the furies over a full lifetime of sailing the seven seas was here in the lighthouse reduced to crying! It was unbelievable!

Under the dateline of December 13th, Marshall recorded, "Ducat still quiet. McArthur praying."

Then the next page, "Gray daylight. Me, Ducat, and McArthur prayed."

Moore found it all impossible to comprehend. In the year he'd been with his companions, never once, even in the worst of gales and pounding seas at the throat of the tower, had he ever known one of them to pray!

Joseph Moore gazed near speechless at the captain.

"One thing be sure, sir. Those men were not praying acause of any storm. No, sir. They could not have had such mortal terror over the winds

76

and tides. Each of them had battled far greater attacks of fierce weather than any such as could have occurred here. There just could not be a storm so frightening as to destroy them—in their minds and in their bodies!"

At that point, the six sailors had covered the entire rocky outpost in their search for the missing lighthouse crew. Not a trace of any of them could be found.

What happened to three stalwart men that seemed to have rendered them frightened beyond reason? First off, it was difficult to understand what storm was referred to in the log, since no bad weather had been recorded for that area. Could a freak local gale have blown into those rocky isles somehow unnoticed by the mainland or nearby islands? The log could not have been talking about the storm that the tender had ridden out for several days, as the log ended on the 15th, eleven days before the tender arrived.

Secondly, even if there had been a bad storm, it could not have panicked the three experienced seamen. And most certainly, not one of the three would have been foolish enough to go down to one of the rocky landings in the midst of a gale. And even in the remote chance that one should have been so misguided, it was absolutely impossible to believe that all *three* would have been so foolhardy as to descend onto slippery, ice-crusted rocks and so be in a position to be washed out to sea and drowned. Moore could not accept such an explanation.

Yet, on the island itself, there wasn't a trace of the three men to be found. They had all—apparently simultaneously—vanished from the place.

Whatever occurred to the three men happened on December 15th after the last entry by Marshall at 1 p.m. ("God is over all"), and that night a passing ship noticed the lighthouse beam was not functioning.

What could have completely eliminated three men from off the rocky face of that remote isle?

Many researchers into sea lore have studied the mystery and written up the tale, but not one of them, any more than the Board of Inquiry established to investigate the puzzle in 1900, has ever been able to supply an answer.

Would the possibility of an interdimensional "door" be the most logical solution, yet the one most overlooked for explaining how whole crews of men have been "sucked away" or "dissolved into air"?

Perhaps a study of the most mysterious crew-vanishing tale ever to be told would be in order. We will cover it in the chapter to follow.

Chapter Six

THE PHILADELPHIA
EXPERIMENT

From the time I moved to the Philadelphia area over thirty years ago, one remarkable tale has kept popping up over and over wherever and whenever persons intrigued with the inexplicables of this world come together to discuss its unsolved mysteries. That is the persistent account of what has come to be called "The Philadelphia Experiment."

Recently with the death of Howard Hughes and the revelation that he had worked undercover for the U.S. government on the development of a supersecret ship, the old Philadelphia Experiment tale has surfaced again. Could there be a connection between the effort to develop a "secret warship" in '43 and the assignment given a Hughes company a few years ago to construct and operate an enormous deep-sea mining ship called *Glomar Explorer*? The latter incorporated a giant claw capable of recovering a sunken Soviet submarine with nuclear warheads—or, if the suspicion of critics is correct—to implant a weapons system on the ocean floor.

The parallels have intrigued old fans of the Philadelphia Experiment story.

Briefly "The Experiment" concerns the claim from a self-labeled "eyewitness" that in October of 1943, during World War II, the U. S. Navy experimented with a destroyer in the Philadelphia Navy Yard. By applying the principles of Einstein's Unified Field theory, the U. S. government attempted to teleport a warship from the Philadelphia Navy Yard to its home dock in Norfolk, Virginia.

The effort, asserted the witness, was successful. The ship not only dematerialized from the Philadelphia dock, then materialized at Norfolk in a matter of minutes, but it dematerialized out of the Virginia dock and re-appeared back in Philadelphia—all, once again, in a few minutes' time.

The achievement relating to the teleportation of matter was all that was hoped for. But it was the effect on the officers and crew of the ship that was the disastrous result of the Philadelphia Experiment, according to the witness. The men were either permanently dematerialized or went mad from the shock of the experience.

What lay behind this story? It has been written up scores of times in newspapers, magazines, and books, but the bold aspects that are inherent in its claims still challenge thought and inspire investigation with an open mind.

Where did it all begin?

It began with the late astrophysicist, astronomer, mathematician, writer, and explorer Morris K. Jessup. Dr. Jessup established several distinguished careers in the 1940's and 1950's. He served as an instructor at the University of Michigan and Drake University in Iowa; then, after receiving his Ph.D. in astrophysics, he turned his scientific know-how to building a refracting telescope in South Africa—the largest in existence in the Southern Hemisphere. Subsequent years found him engaged in exploration along the Amazon River in South America for the U. S. Department of Agriculture; then he went into archeological digging in Mayan ruins of Central America for the Carnegie Institute of Washington.

In 1955 this versatile man turned author as a part of his newest scientific interest—the UFO phenomenon. He wrote a book called *The Case for the UFO*, which was published by the Citadel Press of New York.

In this book, Jessup examined many mysterious puzzles of the world that have presented themselves in the various fields of astronomy, physics, meteorology, and other sciences. He expounded on the problems of interplanetary travel, stating his conviction that the fundamental deterrent to successful space exploration lay in man's insufficient knowledge of the nature of gravity. He called for further research into Einstein's Unified Field theory in which the scientist had hypothesized that electromagnetism and subatomic particles are all related to one set of laws.

It would seem it was this appeal to the world of science to plunge into more extensive research in the Unified Field theory that set off the suffering mind of an eccentric recluse named Carlos Miguel Allende who was, apparently, in Texas at that time. He was a UFO buff and, allegedly, a former seaman during World War II with a traumatic event still burning in his thinking from those years. It seems it was an unforgettable experience and Jessup's book had rekindled its agony.

Accordingly, on January 13, 1956, shortly after Jessup's *The Case for the UFO* had hit the bookstores and library shelves, the author received a letter from Carlos Allende postmarked Gainesville, Texas. The envelope bore the name of the Turner Hotel in Gainesville. The correspondence was a scalding denouncement of the author-scientist for suggesting increased research into the Unified Field theory . . . a dangerous area of experimentation. The letter went on to detail the tragic results of the U. S. government's tinkering around in such universal mysteries as gravity and electromagnetism some thirteen years earlier.

So first unfolded the bizarre story of the Philadelphia Experiment.

It was in 1943, wrote Carlos, during World War

II when he was docked at the Philadelphia Navy Yard, that he became a witness to a supersecret. The U. S. government was engaged in teleportation experiments with a warship!

Young Carlos Allende was a crew member of the S.S. *Andrew Furuseth*,* a Matson Lines Liberty ship out of Norfolk, Virginia. The *Furuseth*, claimed Allende, served as an observation post for the test with the other ship.

The experiment, he stated in his latter to Jessup, was a complete success as far as the destroyer was concerned.

"The result was complete invisibility of the ship, destroyer type, and all its crew, while at sea (October 1943). The field was effective in an oblate spheroidical shape, extending one hundred yards (more or less) out from each beam of the ship. Any person within that sphere became vague in form, but he too observed those persons aboard the ship as though they, too, were of the same state, yet were walking upon nothing. Any person outside that sphere could see nothing save the clearly defined shape of the ship's hull in the

* This ship has mistakenly been misspelled as "Furnseth" in nearly every account of this case. The *Furuseth* has also incorrectly been described as the teleported destroyer. The S. S. *Andrew Furuseth* was a Liberty cargo vessel named for a pioneer in the Maritime Trade Union. Its home base was Richmond, California. However, it was operating in the Atlantic in October of '43. As Allende reported it, the *Furuseth* was the observer ship for the Philadelphia Experiment being conducted on an unnamed destroyer.

water, providing, of course, that the person was just close enough to see, yet barely outside of that field."

Although the experiment with the dematerialization of the destroyer proved to be highly successful (the ship disappearing from Philadelphia and reappearing in a matter of minutes at the Norfolk Navy Yard and back to Philadelphia again), it was in regard to the crew, complained Allende, that the guilt for such an experiment should be weighing heavily on the U. S. government's official and collective conscience. There the results were calamitous. He wrote to Jessup the horrendous details:

"There are only a very few of the original experimental crew left by now, sir. Most went insane, one just walked through his quarters wall in sight of his wife and child and two other crew members were never seen again and two went into flames while carrying common small-boat compasses . . . The experiment was a complete success. The men were complete failures." In a long postscript Allende added that he felt sure the Navy did not realize that the "hyper-field" that rendered the destroyer invisible would affect the men so disastrously. When the results came to light and they discovered that "one or two of the men, visible-within-the-field-to-all-the-others, just walked into nothingness, and nothing could be felt of them, either when the field was turned on or off . . . fears were amassed" and the experimentation ceased.

According to Allende, the effects of the Unified Field secret doings had such far-reaching influences that long after the testing had ceased, the men were suffering the ill results . . . apparently still carrying a "force-field" around them that caused a partially invisible condition. In such a state, some of the crew appeared in a Philadelphia tavern near the Navy Yard, frightening the waitresses out of all sensibility. Subsequently, Allende alleged, one of the Philadelphia newspapers carried an item on the incident "describing the sailors' actions after their initial voyage . . ." (Here I must add that no such newspaper article has ever been tracked down.)

About four months after this first lengthy dissertation had come to Dr. Jessup, a second letter arrived with the home address of New Kensington, Pennsylvania. This was concerned chiefly with ideas or methods for validating the claims given in the first correspondence. Carlos offered to undergo treatments with a truth-serum or hypnotism in order to summon up from his subconscious mind further details that would support his story. Details such as the names and addresses of his crew mates and their service numbers—or their home towns—or even the names and specifics of the waitresses and guests present in the tavern incident—or the name and date of the newspaper item.

Dr. Jessup replied to the letters, not quite sure what to make of his correspondent. Although at first reaction the man seemed to be some sort of complete "kook," there was something, thought

Jessup, arresting about what he had to say. The scientist remembered the fact that during World War II, it was a letter from Dr. Einstein to President Roosevelt detailing the building of an atom bomb, that launched this government into research with the A-Bomb. At that same time, it was possible Einstein's mention of his beginning concepts of a Unified Field theory could have triggered tests with that new idea. It is a fact that the U. S. government was involved in many classified experiments during World War II. Could there have been one related to what Carlos Allende claims to have witnessed?

About the time of the second letter another bizarre twist took place, so goes the story, in the already weird saga of the Philadelphia Experiment. The Office of Naval Research contacted Dr. Jessup and invited him to visit them in the Washington office. Jessup did so, with no little curiosity, and was astounded to be handed a paperback copy of his book.

He looked up, puzzled.

The Navy officer across from him nodded toward the little volume. "This book came to us recently, anonymously. As you will see, it apparently has been read and analyzed by three people who have passed the book back and forth, adding notations each time."

Jessup riffled quickly through the book. The margins were filled with comments, in sets of threes in three different-colored inks! It was not long before Jessup recognized from peculiarities of spelling, punctuation, and style, that one of the commentors, at least (and maybe all), was his old correspondent, Carlos Miguel Allende.

Jessup told the officer about the Allende letters. The man seemed more than interested and asked if his department could have them, adding that it was his intention to have the book, its annotations, and the two letters reproduced in a limited edition for circulation to some of the Navy's top people.

Why, wondered Jessup as he made his way back to his home, was the Navy so interested in what was probably little more than the crazy rantings of a crackpot?

Or was it? He himself had questioned that very assumption. Now, it seemed, so had the U. S. Navy. Later, when he was sent a copy of the department's reproduction, it contained an introduction from the Office of Naval Research that included the statement, "Because of the importance which we attach to the possibility of discovering clues to the nature of gravity, no possible item, however disreputable, from the point of view of classical science, should be overlooked."

How reputable is the now classic tale of "The Philadelphia Experiment"? There is no official response to that question today any more than there was yesterday.

But one final quirk in the case took place on the evening of April 20, 1959. The fifty-nine-year-old Dr. Morris K. Jessup climbed into his station wagon in Dade County Park, near Coral Gables, Florida, pulled a hose attached to the car's exhaust pipe into the closed car with him, and breathed deep. It was the end of Morris K. Jessup, key figure in one of the strangest stories ever to circulate around the world.

What happened to Carlos Miguel Allende (sometimes referred to as Carl Allen)? Two researchers and writers concerned with the Experiment case have written the following concluding comments relating to the whereabouts of the mysterious Allende:

Vincent Gaddis, who covered the story in his book, *Invisible Horizons*, states that one investigator tracked down the rural home address of Carlos in New Kensington, Pennsylvania, only to find the farmhouse vacant. Neighbors he queried stated that there had been a man living there by the name of Carlos or Carl. He had been rooming there with an elderly couple. One morning, however, reported the neighbors, a truck had rolled up to the farmhouse, loaded all the furniture in it, and rumbled away. They never saw any of the three people next door again.

Investigator and writer Brad Steiger, in his book, *Mysteries of Time and Space*, tells of a strange incident that occurred shortly after the publication of an earlier book in which he examined the Experiment tale (*The Allende Letters*). A large UFO group published in their newsletter the story that one Carlos Miguel Allende had appeared at their offices with the down-at-the-mouth recounting of how he had learned of Steiger's assignment to write up Carlos's correspondence with

This photo was snapped hurriedly by the occupant of the car in the center of the picture who had quickly gotten out of the vehicle and snapped the shot of the UFO, catching it just before it slipped out of view. Was the whirring object from a Parallel Universe?

An old newspaper photo of the New York Heiress, Dorothy Arnold, who vanished off Fifth Avenue on December 12, 1910. Did she slip abruptly into another dimension?

Judge Joseph Force Crater, one of the most mysterious solitary vanishers of all time. After dining with friends at Billy Haas' restaurant on West 4th Street in New York City on the evening of August 6th 1930, the judge stepped outside, hailed a taxi, climbed in and was never seen again.

A master of mystery-story writing, the renowned Ambrose Bierce took a trip around Christmastime in 1913. He never returned and no word was ever heard from him again. Like so many other vanishers, he seemed to "step into another world."

A lenticular cloud crowns Mount Shasta in California.
Do strange forces focus at its peak?

A Tibetan lama, member of a mystic order who claim the ability to walk in the air. Do such men possess "out of this world" energies?

(Left) Considered the greatest dancer who ever lived, Vaslov Nijinsky, achieved not only remarkable elevation but the ability to *sustain* it beyond any scientific plausibility. Was this unique dancer capable of generating a force that counteracted gravitation?

The Great Pyramid at Giza in Egypt built over 4,500 years ago. It still stands as the most massive structure ever erected by man. Did its builders avail themselves of some kind of force or power known to them, unknown to modern man?

In 1798 Napoleon and his forces defeated the fighting horsemen of the Turkish governor, Mourad Bey, in sight of the pyramids. Awed by the imposing Great Pyramid, Napoleon visited it on October 12th. Reputedly, he saw a vision within its walls. Does the pyramid shape generate strange forces?

The magnificent gold mummy mask of King Tutankhamen discovered when archaeologists unearthed the treasure tomb in 1923. Tales of a curse defied in this excavation have rung down through the decades. This mask is on tour of the United States from 1976–1979.

The mummy case of the temple priestess of Amen-Ra. Long considered a "haunted case", this ancient Egyptian relic can be seen today in the Egyptian wing of the British Museum in London. The dark eyes have been called "glowing" and have been said to be "death-dealing."

Jessup and of how he had begged the author not to publish it, etc, but that Steiger was iron-hearted and ignored him and what could a little man do against the powers of the pen and a large publishing firm?

Steiger expressed his displeasure with the fact that neither he nor his publisher had ever received a call or a letter from a soul in an effort to verify the story which, was, Steiger clearly states, completely untrue. No person by the name of Carlos Allende had ever approached him or his publisher.

So, today, as over the past decades, the name of Allende is still shrouded in mystery, confusion, and a great deal of wonder. As is the fantastic account of the Philadelphia Experiment.

Those of us who mused over it twenty years ago are still intrigued today with the possible inherent clues that may be stored in those Allende papers.

Think about such statements of Allende's as "One or two of their men . . . just walked into nothingness . . ." Do we do ourselves or our fellow man any service by turning serious consideration away in the light of what we have seen and discussed in this book already? Is the truth to be uncovered as the key to the Allende mystery not related to UFO's or outer space per se, as so many believe, but to that ever-present theme of a parallel Universe? Could there have been a force-field created by Navy experimenters over thirty years ago that interacted with the forces of our invisible partner? Did such a force remove several members of the crew or, more to the point, propel them into another dimension?

Did a destroyer that day in 1943 dematerialize from its material atomic structure, vanish into a dimension of another space-time, and return? Did some of the crew slip back and forth between "worlds," causing partial invisibility? Did some step into that other dimension completely and permanently? Are they housed there to this day in time, along with the other vanished ones of our planet?

If the men of the Philadelphia Experiment, like those other vanished ones of our planet, have gone into an alternate Universe, where could such a dimension be? Of what is it constituted? One of the most repeated suggestions heard from scientists puzzling over the parallel Universe idea is that it is another dimension of time.

Can there be a time other than that which we know and govern our lives by? We will examine the possibility in the next chapter.

Chapter Seven

IS TIME THE TUNNEL FROM HERE TO THERE?

The old Newtonian concept of a Universe of three-dimensional space completely independent of time crumbled before Einstein's Theory of Relativity in the early years of this century. Physics now recognizes a Universe in which space and time are indissolubly linked. None of us on Earth are standing still. We are all moving through space and because we are moving, we are growing old at a less rapid rate than if the Earth were standing still. The astronauts, soaring through space, age less rapidly than we back on Earth. In other words, the faster one travels, the more time slows down. Everything is relative, and so the basis of

Einstein's theory establishes the fact that space and time are interrelated and woven together—inextricably.

For example, man looks up to the sky today and sees a star exploding and at the same time realizes the event took place millions of years ago and that he is seeing something that actually no longer is in existence. What is he witnessing? The present, or the past? What is happening is the awesome truth that an event of a distant past is taking place in the present. The light from the explosion has required a length of time to reach man's vision that has far exceeded the life of the star matter that emitted the light. Space has affected time. One cannot exist without the other. Time is no longer the traditional concept, an independent factor. It is part and parcel of space. The Universe incorporates a space-time continuum. All of which forces us to review our concepts of time as a single along-one-line-type of procession. If space is everywhere at once, then likewise, would not time have the same characteristic? Why should we think it can occur only in a sequence pattern? Is not this traditional concept a construct of man's own creation—a division of time into successive moments for practical advantages—a pattern he imposes upon time which time itself does not possess? Clocks record our sense of time, but they do not make it. Clearly, man has made it. He has determined that a certain interval elapses between events and so he measures it by instruments and then pronounces that the present event is *now* and all that happened before is the *past* and all that is yet to occur is the *future*. Such reasoning is beginning to appear a very faulty one.

One of the first men to tell us so was the late English scientist, J. W. Dunne, who designed the first British military plane. Today he is much better known for his revolutionary theories on time. His work, *An Experiment with Time*, is a classic in its field.

An aeronautical engineer with a great interest in physics and mathematics, Dunne became absorbed in the 1930's with Einstein's Theory of Relativity. He set about to construct a theory of time that would fit in with Einstein's relativistic concepts. What he came up with is roughly this: if time is a series that flows forward, then there must be another kind of time (in which it flows) that measures *it*.

From this thesis he went on to suggest that human beings also have several levels. There is the first "Me" who lives and experiences in this life and then another "Me" who is conscious of the first "Me." Such an awareness becomes manifest whenever one has the thought of "Myself." It is the second and detached "I" or "Me" who exists, not in time as we know it, but in Time Two. This "Me" is able to look backwards and forward in time.

There is the one "Me," asserted Dunne, who goes through life dully and in a sequence of events, and then there is the second "Me" which observes. That second "Me" Dunne called "mind." This mind—and all other men's minds—are small aspects of a single Universal Mind.

The first "Me," the passive one, Dunne felt, has a narrow choice of what it can look at—merely the events of its mortal life. The second "Me" or mind is not so restricted. It reflects; it judges and discriminates. It is a broad observer. When we are asleep the second mind is particularly free. It occupies itself glancing at the past and future as well as the present.

It is the second and detached "Me" who exists in Time Two and is able to look forward and backwards in Time, unlike the limited first "Me" which is restricted to mortal time, Time One.

To sum it up, Dunne argued for a four-dimensional "serial" Universe in which the inner or second "Me," particularly in sleep, is free of the waking restrictions of viewing time from moment to moment in a one-directional flow. It slips into another dimension of space-time awareness which allows that person to travel freely through time either backwards or forward.

According to this theory, time is related to awareness. I myself can testify to experiencing such a stepping-out-of-time (as we know it). In a broader sense, the traditional sense of time ceased for me. Let me explain.

One day when my daughter was in high school a very important event was coming up which she was particularly anxious to attend. It was scheduled for afternoon shortly after the closing hour of her school day, which was at three o'clock. For days prior to the big day, she mentioned repeatedly to me the importance of my being at school to pick her up *promptly* at three p.m. Upon the arrival of the day in question she pulled away from me with the final declaration. "Remember, please, be at school on the dot of three!"

I watched the clock closely throughout my afternoon work, and on the stroke of two-thirty I picked up my car keys from the piano top and started for the front door. I took a look at my watch and checked it against our never-failing grandfather clock. I needed a half-hour to make the trip down to the school (which was several towns and miles away). Just at that instant, my telephone rang. It was a neighbor in a town down the pike who was in distress. She needed my help desperately to pick up her daughter and take her to a hospital several towns below me. Her voice showed her need. All I could do was assure her I'd do it.

As I pulled out of my drive and steamed off down the main road, I felt torn with distress. I seemed to be faced with an impossible task: devotion to two needs that I felt I must respond to yet no way to fulfill my obligations to two different people in two different directions within a short space of time.

I found the girl (who was visiting in a house that took me some time to locate), then got her to the hospital as fast as I could. After that deed was accomplished, I hurriedly glanced at my watch, then up at the hospital reception room clock. Both said three minutes before three!

I got behind my wheel with a panicky heart. What would my daughter say? I had failed her! I would be so late, and I had *promised*—

In the middle of that self-chastisement, I mentally stopped myself and took stock of the situation as I started off in the direction of her school about six miles away. Why should I feel so sure I would be failing her? Why should either she or I suffer for the deed I had done? It was a good deed. How can one really be punished for doing good? Actually, one cannot, I reasoned. Good begets good. Somehow, that fine moment would be followed by another fine moment. And so on.

I drove along in a new and remarkable calm. I felt as though I were serenely gliding above all traffic—over all obstacles—without any fear, hurry, or incapacitation. I began to think about time. There was no such thing as "keeping time" out in the Universe. The only testimony that there was such a thing as a limited twenty-four-hour period was a clock. I wasn't bound to perform good within such mortal limits as my wristwatch or a hall clock might dictate. I lived and moved in a Universe outside of this matter collection of worlds, I was sure.

I drove along, serenely peaceful. I didn't speed; I didn't push through any lights. I didn't even experience a faster heartbeat. I wasn't the slightest bit distressed as I drove up into the school yard.

I was amazed to find the driveway empty of buses that I felt would surely be pulling away full to the brim by now. There wasn't a sign of a pupil waiting outside. Not a glimmer of my daughter I expected to see waiting by the front door.

I parked and stepped quickly up the main stairs into the foyer of the school. Just as I walked into an empty hallway, the clock on the wall chimed three. I looked up, amazed. At that precise moment, the principal came out of his office to my right. I pointed up at the clock and said, "I think your clock is very slow—"

The principal glanced up; then checked his wristwatch. He shook his head, staring at me in surprise, and answered. "No, it's not. It's exactly right. It's three o'clock." As he walked off, I looked down at my own wristwatch, convinced it had to read about three-fifteen, at least. I stared in shock. My watch also read three o'clock!

I backed out and returned to my car. In seconds, my daughter was running out and I drove her down to her appointed place—all in good time. She made the event exactly when she wished to and was superbly happy. I, too, was superbly happy that day and many days to follow. The experience was such a treasure and such a miracle to me that I did not dare share it with anyone for a long time afterwards. People would think me mad, I thought. Somehow I had traveled a ten-to-fifteen-minute time interval in three minutes! Somehow, time had stood still for me here on earth. For a brief period I had stepped into another Universe. I have always felt it was a spiritual Universe where good measures time, not clocks.

Is time, then, perhaps the "tunnel" through

which we may move from this world into a twin universe? And are there special spots on earth where one might be particularly apt to find such openings? In the next chapter we will search for all possible exits!

Chapter Eight

THIS WAY TO THE
NEAREST EXIT

Are there certain areas on our earth which, for some reason indeterminate at this time, provide multidimensional access to our reality from another Universe or Universes?

Some investigators like Brad Steiger feel that there are. This writer-researcher refers to them as "Window Areas." (*Saga*, May 1976). The late Ivan Sanderson, world-famous geologist, zoologist, and botanist, discussed such strange zones in an article for *Fate* magazine (September 1963). He wrote, "It appears not everything is anchored down quite as properly as it should be according to Newtonian principles of gravity (on our earth)

. . . places where the pebbles don't seem to be lying on the ground or gravitically pressed to it as they should. . . . One such (is) a glacial circle at the head of the Songe or the Nord Fjord in Norway. There is another in the vast volcanic crater of Kintamani on Bali in Indonesia . . . things come loose . . . and they take off . . . to where?" Sanderson answers that question with the possibility: "Into another space-time continuum?" Such areas of irregularity are known as "Vortexes."

In the October 1973 *Psychology Today* article mentioned earlier, psychologist Dr. Stanley Krippner was asked, "What is a vortex?"

Dr. Krippner replied, "It's a location where people and other living things and objects do not behave as they ordinarily would. Individuals who go into some of the natural vortexes such as the one near Mount Shasta (California) claim that they enter a different state of consciousness. . . ."

The Mount Shasta area has long been regarded as a mind-boggling zone. Its strange powers were known centuries ago to the Indians of northern California. They are still revered by many sects and organizations such as "The Radiant School" which thrives at the foot of Mount Shasta, serenely promulgating its philosophy that the beautiful mountain is a "magnetic center" and an inspiration to man's physical senses and an awareness of his "Higher Self."

What is there about Mount Shasta that affects men's minds? No one has ever come up with an answer. Is it a "dimensional window" of some kind?

What is it about an unusual spot north of Shasta in Oregon known as "The Oregon Vortex" that makes *it* unique? Dubbed one of America's most mysterious spots, the Oregon Vortex, also, like Shasta, was familiar to the Indians. They called it "The Forbidden Ground." Even their horses were sensitive to the peculiar magnetics of the vortex and refused to step near it.

This vortex's peculiarities are endlessly challenging. Located in Gold Hill about nineteen miles out of Medford, close to Sardine Creek, the vortex is an area about one hundred and sixty-five feet in diameter. Within this radius strange gravitical tricks seem to occur. Right in the heart of this mysterious circle stands an old wooden shack, formerly an assay office for a mining company. Originally, the shed stood atop the hill above the vortex spot but many years ago it slipped down the slope and twisted to a standstill right in the heart of the mystery area. It is within this structure that most of the amazing things characteristic of the gravity-defying vortex seem to occur.

A person entering the hut finds himself leaning at an angle of about 10° toward the center of the vortex circle. A broom braced for support will not stand upright but leans at a sharp angle to the floor. A twenty-eight-pound steel ball hangs *at an angle* from a chain suspended from an overhead beam.

Although any house, distorted by a fall down a

slope, can give the illusion that gravity has gone berserk because of the effect of tilting floors, doors, and windows to the eye, this house of mystery remains more than just a twisted structure. There is much more than the anti-gravity effects just mentioned.

For example, if two men of equal height stand, one in front of the other, a short distance apart, to the observer the man in the more northerly position will seem taller than the other, even if he is standing farther away from the observer! Contrary to the laws of perspective, this is an astonishing fact and must be seen to be believed. One explanation for this shrinking effect has been offered by several scientists studying the Oregon Vortex. They say the area is a circular electromagnetic whirlpool of force, making objects and people lean toward magnetic north, causing water to flow uphill and possibly in the case of the shrinking man, actually bending light rays much the same way light is altered by a lens, creating the smaller visual image. Other scientists have suggested that the strange vortex force-field compacts molecules to the point that reduced forms and objects actually are smaller.

One scientist, a skeptic named Herbert B. Nichols, some years ago, took a carpenter's level and a plumb bob with him into the shack and he declared that there were no strange forces at work; viewers were merely victims of optical illusions.

But such pat analysis does not answer everything odd that goes on in the vortex. There are a multitude of weird effects that cannot be solved so easily. Cigarette smoke swirls into spirals on its own. Compasses don't work inside the hut or out. A light meter will give one reading within the shack and another outside. Birds will not fly within the mysterious area. Trees growing within the circle will grow limbs that droop and lean toward magnetic north. Indeed, something outside of optical illusion is causing these oddities, Oregon Vortex supporters point out.

The Oregon Vortex does not stand alone as a possible link to a parallel universe.

Could a strange force-field similar to that of the Oregon Vortex be "penetrating" our universe in a "window zone" such as Ecuador's Galapagos Islands in the Pacific?

These thirteen islands are inhabited by some of the most remarkable and awesome creatures in the world . . . seals, iguanas, giant tortoises, lizards, and scores of rare bird species. Twelve of these Pacific isles are just what one would expect of a tropical, out-of-the-world chain . . . they are covered with lush green vegetation and filled with the songs of birds. But not all of them. One island is totally different from the others. That is Baltra.

Separated from Santa Cruz Island by a channel some fifty feet wide and three feet deep, Baltra is a strange sea-fellow. Unlike the others, it has no living vegetation. It is called a "dead island." Its dried tree stumps boast no branches or leaves. Nothing here seems to grow. Unlike the others, Baltra gets no rainfall. Considering its proximity to Santa Cruz, of identical height, this is truly remarkable.

During World War II, the U. S. maintained an air base at Baltra. The men based there reported a variety of peculiarities. One man, Francis Wagner, still recalls the strange effect of standing at the edge of the channel watching a heavy tropical rain beat down over Santa Cruz, then pass over Baltra without dropping so much as one drop on his head. About one hundred feet out to the ocean on the other side, it started pouring again!

Wagner remembers the strange experience of standing at the channel's edge. "You can see it raining in the channel, even; but just as it gets about halfway across, it stops!"

This former airman also recalls the weird magnetic effects of Baltra. A normal compass held in the hand may abruptly spin so fast that you think the instrument will fall apart! Then the needle will suddenly stop, point in any direction it may choose, and freeze there. "You can even put a magnet to your compass," Wagner states, "in order to hold the needle in a set position, but some power comes over your magnetification, and promptly the needle goes its merry way to any direction it wishes!" This same malfunctioning affected the aircraft, too. On take-off, it was common for the tower to tell a pilot, "You are cleared for take-off. Disregard your compass till you are off the island!"

"On any other island that would sound crazy. But not on Baltra!" declares Wagner.

Then the former airman can go on to discuss a "feeling" one gets on this unusual island. "It is hard to say what I want to about this feeling," Wagner wrote me a short time ago. "Let me put it this way: you feel you are a part of something like a Great Plan. You are a small part of a big picture." Wagner even asked some of the other men about this strange sensation. Many agreed, "Yeah, you feel funny for a few days, but it will go away." With Francis Wagner it didn't go away. Only when he went swimming or fishing or riding the backs of sea turtles far out did the strangeness go away. But the moment he set foot back on Baltra, the old feeling of oddness returned.

Is there a "force field" unknown to us, focused at Baltra much as it appears to be in the Oregon Vortex or on Mount Shasta?

"I can tell you there's a force there on that island as strong as a brick wall. I have stood watching birds fly across the island and suddenly stop with an impact as though they'd struck a glass partition. And I think they did—an invisible wall of a force of some kind," concludes Francis Wagner.

Does such a force operate at various times in various places on our earth and affect the thinking of men like Wagner and often, too, his behavior?

Back in Oregon once more, we can take a look at one of the strangest cases of disappearance ever to occur . . . at Rogue River National Forest Campground, one mile from Copper, Oregon, not far from the California border. On September 5, 1974, the family of Richard Cowden went camping for Labor Day weekend. The group included Richard, his wife, Belinda, and their two children, David, five, and the infant Melissa. On Sunday morning, Richard showed up in the local store at Copper to buy some milk. It was about 9 a.m. That was the last ever seen of any of the Cowdens. Sunday night the family was to come for dinner at Richard's mother's and stay till morning. No one ever showed up.

Finally, the local authorities were called. One trooper, Lee Rickson, said afterwards, "That camp sure was spooky. Even the milk was still on the table." It was, said the investigators, as though suddenly the whole family walked away—with no fuss or preparation. Cooking utensils still rested on a tree stump. Richard's wallet and his wife's purse were found intact. Fishing rods still leaned against a tree, and the family car was still parked just above the campsite. There was no sign of a struggle or of any disturbance of any kind.

Could the whole family have been kidnapped? For what reason? None of the family members were wealthy. Would they have all fallen into an abandoned mine shaft? Hardly could all of them have disappeared in such a fashion, and especially since Richard knew the area well. Search parties combed a twenty-five-mile radius without turning up a single clue.

Could some unknown force have acted upon the whole Cowden family . . . driving them somewhere, somehow?

Mountains seem to have such a characteristic . . . a force character that can affect man, both in mind and body. Like Shasta—and the Vortex Hill —there is the peculiar Mount Glastonbury in Vermont. People seem to vanish from this mount without a trace or a reason. Are they all *going* somewhere?

Glastonbury consists largely of untraveled sections peppered with small villages. Founded in the 1760's, Glastonbury town never had a population exceeding two hundred and fifty, and that occurred only in the last century when some of the first-growth timber was being cut and scores of transient lumbermen swelled the local numbers. Since 1937, Glastonbury has been home to no more than half a dozen people.

But it was for a period of about a decade from the mid-1950's to the mid-1960's that the mountain became a mystery zone. The particular "avenue of disappearance" in this rocky, mountainous area is the Long Trail (an extension of the Appalachian Trail) which traverses the high land down the center of Vermont. It has been on or near this trail that so many people have vanished over a period of time without leaving a trace.

First on record was a seventy-five-year-old hunting guide named Middie Rivers. He vanished while on a hunting trip in the area of Woodford, just south of Glastonbury, in the 1950s. Not a vestige of his body, his boots, or his gun was ever located.

A few months later, a Bennington College student, Paula Weldon, went hiking on the trail and never returned. Nothing was ever found to indicate foul play. She just seemed, as one local townsperson put it, "to go up in smoke."

Not long afterwards a three-month-old baby vanished in this area and was never found.

Close on the heels of this and the Weldon girl's disappearance, eight-year-old Paul Jepson was left in the family truck for a few minutes, and when his father returned the truck was empty. Bloodhounds were brought, and the dogs took off toward the trail. They sniffed and trotted at a rapid pace, then suddenly stopped. They would go no farther. The point where they marked the end of the boy's trail was the exact spot where Paula Weldon had last been seen!

Shortly after the Jepson incident, two more vanishings occurred. Young Frances Christman went for a walk, and she was never seen again. Close on her final act, a Martha Jones followed suit, walking into a kind of "Glastonbury Oblivion," as had all the rest before her.

Around 1962 a Richard Bentley of Sunderland (a town just north of Glastonbury) took off into the mountains to search for wild ginseng, highly prized in this age of interest in natural health-giving food and herbs. (For centuries ginseng has been considered by Orientals as more precious than gold.)

Sometime in late May or early June, Bentley decided to gather the roots. It was a hunt he enjoyed, for the mountains were his pleasure. He'd spent all his life hunting and fishing all over Mount Glastonbury. Last seen just over the township line in Manchester, Richard Bentley, with his hunting dogs keeping stride with him, stalked off headed for the trail. It was his last hunt. Bentley never returned home. Unbelieving that such an experienced outdoorsman could just disappear, scores of neighbors and friends joined in a thorough search. Two local industries in the town of Arlington, the Hale Company (a furniture factory) and Mack Molding (a plastic manufacturer), closed down for several days in order that their employees could aid in the search for Bentley. But not a sign of the hunter or his dogs ever showed up from that day to this.

In the *National Examiner* of April 12, 1976, journalist Bill Campbell discussed some of the foregoing disappearances in an article on strange vanishings. Near the conclusion he asks the oft-repeated inquiry: Is there (at Glastonbury) a "window or a doorway to another dimension?" Have the "people who vanished stepped into another world invisible to our eyes?" In other words, is Mount Glastonbury a major "exit" to our parallel universe?

Some researchers into the most active "exits" on our planet feel Pennsylvania may be the choicest area in which to find an "opening" into another dimension. Certainly, the state boasts one of the most colorful and legendary spots of mystery in our country . . . the area known locally as "The Black Forest."

This vast acreage of cool, deep-green woods and lively streams sprinkled with hamlets here and there lies in the north central portion of Pennsylvania. The original wooded area covered nearly thirty million acres. It was thick with conifers, pines, and hemlocks—all common to our country's more northern climes. Antedating William Penn's arrival in this region in 1681 by many centuries, much of the white pine stretches were of ancient lineage. They are still existent in places and are known as the "primeval white pine stands" of the Black Forest.

This is North-Branch-of-the-Susquehanna-Country, and it is peaceful and beautiful . . . and a centuries-old aid to man. It has been estimated that these woods over the years have yielded nearly three hundred billion board feet of timber!

The German settlers revered these woods as they did their homeland's Black Forest. Hence, its name. The early comers to this area—all of them—recognized the valuable "storehouse" the forest provided of natural resources to sustain existence. From these woods the settlers got logs for their homes, rails to fence their lands, ashes from burned timber to render valuable potash, bark for leather tanning, lumber for buildings, charcoal for ironmaking, timber for staves and barrels, and wood for household utensils and farm implements. In short, the forest was the early settler's life.

But in the centuries to come a new aspect of the Black Forest was to unfold: it seemed to develop into being an exit point for human beings from off the face of this globe!

One of the first residents of the forest region to note and record such disappearances was the late writer-historian, Robert Lyman, Sr., of Coudersport in Potter County at the northern border of the Black Forest. For years, Lyman tracked down and investigated a score of strange vanishings from that wooded area. He wrote of them in two slim pamphlets entitled, *Forbidden Land* (an early Indian name for the Black Forest) and a follow-up volume called *Amazing Indeed* (one of my most cherished possessions).

Lyman opens his chapter in *Amazing Indeed* called "Lost and Never Found" with:

"Since earliest times, hundreds of persons from little children to old men have been lost in our Black Forest. . . . Scores have vanished without a trace. Their sudden disappearances remain as great mysteries." Then the historian goes on to recount the vanishings of such oldtime forest inhabitants as the "Jones Boy" who went to gather the cows for milking one evening as was his custom. A short time later, the cows came back, but not the boy. Later, a young girl named Catherine Gray went to seek out some lost cows for her parents and never returned. A swamp in McKean County is named for the place where she disappeared.

Then there is the fascinating case of young Peter Handwerk. Shortly after the close of the Civil War, seven-year-old Peter was tending a cow in a small pasture area near the town of Germania. Toward dusk, the cow began to meander off toward the wooded area. Peter hurried after her to urge her back into the pasture, but he had difficulty in turning her around. A passing neighbor spotted the boy in his futile attempts and called out to him to let the cow go; it was getting dark and he'd best be getting home. The boy, reported the neighbor later, seemed to pay no mind to the instructions and continued chasing the cow into the woods. Peter never did make it home. The neighbors and townsfolk of Germania aided the distraught family in a far-and-wide search. They never found so much as a button from his shirt.

In 1898 a small girl vanished in very similar fashion. She was searching for some lost cows of her father's near Carter Camp and never came back home. Not a trace of her was turned up, nor any clue as to what might have become of her.

Still another child vanished, this time in 1910. It was on a typical spring day in April that seven-year-old Earl Adams picked up his fishing pole and entered the woods with three pals to go fishing. Somehow the youth got separated from his companions. They turned when they got to the stream to find Earl was not with them. The three boys searched for him and called his name as far around the area as they could comb themselves. Finally, they gave up and returned home near dark without the boy. Earl's parents thrashed through every foot of woods in the area around

Kane where they lived in McKean County. Not a sign of the child was forthcoming. Searching parties joined the hunt using bloodhounds, but all to no avail. They never located little Earl Adams or ever learned what had befallen him that had removed him so utterly and completely. Even private detectives hired by the father could find nothing.

In a strange coincidence, on that same day of April 16, 1910, another youth, Michael Steffan of Ludlow, several miles from the Adams's house, vanished from his home. Hundreds of neighbors searched for him also, but with no success. Even a posted reward brought no clue. Five years earlier, it was recalled, near Medix Run, a little boy who had gone trout fishing by himself never returned home. Not a sign of his fishing pole or his basket had ever turned up. Now young Earl Adams and Michael Steffan, also of the Black Forest, had joined this boy in a Never-Never-Land that no one could explain. All they knew was that it seemed to be linked with this deep wooded area of north central Pennsylvania.

Was it—and *is* it—an exit to a parallel Universe, invisible and unknown to the inhabitants of the Black Forest—both then and now?

The sudden exiting of individuals continued through subsequent years. On the 30th of November in 1933 a hunter who took off for a trek through the Trout Run and Hammersley Fork section to look for game never came back to camp. In 1941, a young boy disappeared a few miles north of the town of Emporium in the heart of the Black Forest. No trace of him was ever discovered. A big Texas-bred man by the name of Art Wiseman just vanished one day in 1956 leaving behind a new jeep, a fine gun collection worth about three thousand dollars, and all his clothing and a stack of wages due him. No one ever figured out what happened to the two-hundred-pound Texan. Had he gotten lost? Murdered? Or did he slip, like all the others, into another world?

On October 31, 1964, David Stevens of Altoona, Pennsylvania, had a hunting camp in Little Moore's Run in Homer Township. His brother Edward, of Pittsburgh, was with him. On that Saturday morning David and Edward and a friend, John Barker from Ohio, all went into the woods to hunt squirrels. They separated, each covering a different area. At 4 p.m. they were to meet again in the road. When the time arrived, only Edward and John showed up. They waited an hour for David. No David. Finally, they went back in the woods and searched until dark. No luck. It was incredible to them that David could have gotten lost. He was an experienced woodsman and hunter and knew that forest area well.

Eventually the two men sought the aid of Claude Reno, a forest ranger. Reno arrived with a small search party. They combed the woods until one o'clock Sunday morning without unearthing a trace. Then fifty more men joined the hunt crisscrossing the area all that day. By Monday the searchers had increased to seventy under the direction of two district game wardens. Still no success. Bloodhounds from the state police academy at Hershey were brought in, but they, too, found nothing.

The Allegheny Civil Defense Rescue Unit offered their aid with a "weasel" for transportation and walkie-talkies for communication. All in vain. For ten days the search continued, but eventually had to be abandoned. Not the smallest clue as to David's fate ever turned up. He, along with all the others, was gone for good.

But the strangest and strongest clue as to what is going on in the Black Forest may be that unequaled case of a man in Hammersley Fork, Clinton County, shortly after the Civil War. A group of men were clustered on the porch of the Jake Hammersley Hotel, discussing the day's events, when suddenly they all became aware of a man approaching them from the direction of South Forks, north of them on Kettle Creek.

The man was walking unsteadily and was talking to himself. He eventually passed by the hotel verandah, paying no attention to anyone and still talking to himself. About six hundred feet beyond the hotel, he suddenly paused in the middle of the road and began to scream, "Let me go, damn you; let me go!" And before the astonished eyes of the men on the porch, the man abruptly rose in the air!

The group of witnesses hurried down the verandah steps and rushed to the spot where the man had last been standing. Seconds later, they were joined by another group of men who had seen the same incident and had come running to the place also. All in all, about twenty men were assembled in the middle of the road gazing upward at the disappearing form of the strange man until all sign of him was gone from sight!

According to Lyman, the man's footsteps in the dirt road ended right where he was seen to levitate. On one side of the spot was a cornfield and on the other a sandbar and a creek. Where could a man go? Nowhere that anyone could see. The men searched the neighboring woods and fields but never found a trace or heard tell any more of the stranger who disappeared into thin air right before their very eyes.

The townspeople there still tell the story to this day. I spoke to one man, William Schoonober, at Hammersley Fork a short time ago. He told me he had heard the tale many times as a boy from the late Hi Cranmer, who in turn had heard it from an old man who was one of the men on the hotel porch. There can be no doubt of the authenticity of the incident—so many witnessed it—say the townspeople.

All of which leaves us with the startling possibility that perhaps, in the Black Forest, more easily than anywhere else on earth, man can make his treacherous and irreversible transit to that unknown and parallel Universe.

Is it a two-way transit? Can people come to us as well as leave us? Let us see in the chapter to follow.

Chapter Nine

WHERE DID THEY COME FROM?

Accounts of strange appearances of out-of-this-world beings abound all over our globe. One of the weirdest and most inexplicable occurred in England during the Victorian age. He was called "The Jumping Man." He was first spotted in 1837 by Jane Alsop, a young girl who lived near the docks of the Thames. One night she heard the bell ring at the gate in front of the house. She opened the front door to see a tall form wrapped in a long cloak. She raised her candle to see the person better when, with a startled howl, the visitor reared back. His cloak fell from his shoulders, and she saw a man dressed in a tight-fitting jumpsuit. His head was encased in a globe-shaped covering through which she could see a pair of eyes burning.

The young girl screamed, and the man ran off into the night. The local police were notified, but no one took the story seriously until a young man who worked in a butcher shop nearby came forth and told the same story. He had seen his two sisters attacked by such a man who, upon his arrival, had hastily run away, jumping in one clean bound over a brick wall that ran down the length of the alley. The wall was over fourteen feet high!

Nothing more was seen or heard of "The Jumping Man" until 1845. That year reports started pouring in from the Ealing and Hanwell districts of London. A weird figure was repeatedly seen jumping over hedges and walls. Then nothing more until an outbreak in the 1860's and '70's—accounts that placed the Jumper in Warwickshire, Lancashire, Lincolnshire, Surrey, Worcestershire, and Middlesex counties—all detailing the sighting of a man who leaped over fences and hedges more than twenty and thirty feet high.

In 1877 the Jumping Man nearly outdid himself. He appeared to two sentries at a British Army post near Aldershot. The men were on duty at a powder-magazine storehouse when the strange leaper appeared bounding up and down, an odd "bubble" on his shoulers. Both guards shot at the leaping form, but there seemed to be no effect on the intruder. In panic, the two soldiers dropped their guns and ran. The subsequent court-martial testimony duplicated the account given to the police by Jane Alsop over forty years earlier.

Later that year residents of Newport reported an incident in which the leaping creature was seen on a thatched roof, just standing there, gazing down. When the neighbors assembled to look at him, the strange being leaped from the roof right over the crowd and vanished in twenty-foot-high leaps.

In 1904, the weird man was spotted for the last reported time. It was in Liverpool. In midday the man was seen by hundreds of townspeople bounding airily up and down the streets of William Henry and Stitt, then over a row of houses on to High Street, and finally in a final burst of display, he made a gigantic leap back over the slate roofs of Salisbury Street and was gone from view—forever. He was never reported again. The London *Morning Post* of October 29, 1929, reviewed the odd sightings in a piece on the Jumping Man case. He was "clearly no ordinary mortal," the article stated, "if, indeed, he were of this world at all."

Appearances equally strange as the Jumping Man have been noted throughout the years by various witnesses all over the world. One of the most inexplicable happened in Spain in August of 1887. John Macklin wrote about it in an article for *Grit* newspaper (December 1966). The writer tells us that it was on the afternoon during harvest time near the village of Banjos that two small children came timidly out of a cave and started walking across the field toward some harvesters sitting eating their lunch. The workers nearly dropped their loaves and wine bottles on seeing the children, for their skin was green!

When they stood directly in front of the harvesters, the children began to talk. It was in an incomprehensible language no one present had ever heard before. And the clothes the children wore were of a substance utterly unlike any fabric used here on earth.

In time a priest from Barcelona arrived to investigate the unusual case of the unidentifiable children. The whole thing was so incredible, he eventually sat down and put the incident into writing. "I have been so convinced by what I heard that I felt obliged to accept the fact even if incapable of understanding it and of making any explanation with the power of intellect."

Writer Macklin goes on to detail exactly what had taken place: "The frightened children . . . were brought to the magistrate . . . He took the hand of the child and stroked it: the colour stayed green, so undoubtedly it was part of the pigment. He offered them food but they did not eat. . . . The magistrate observed that the facial features . . . seemed rather like those of the Negro; the eyes were almond-shaped and deep in the sockets. The children stayed five days . . . without eating and were clearly growing weaker . . . they got the chance one day to eat some beans which they both devoured madly. . . .

"But the starvation had seriously harmed the boy . . . he grew weaker and died a month after his appearance. The girl, however, grew better and became later a domestic servant in . . . (the magistrate's) house; the green colour got less noticeable . . . After some months she was able to say a few words in Spanish and even give some explanation of her arrival—but this only served to deepen the mystery . . . she had come from a land where there was no sun, a country of eternal twilight . . . How had she reached Earth? She said the only thing she could remember was a very loud noise after which she was taken up and found herself with her brother on a harvest field. The girl," Macklin concludes, "lived another five years and was then buried with her brother. It is indeed a strange story . . . the documents concerning the case exist, together with all the evidence given under oath by witnesses who saw, touched and questioned the children."

In his book, *Not of This World*, Peter Kolosimo relates the story of the green children, quoting also from the Macklin article. He sees the incident as a spur for "researches into the fourth dimension of a world existing side by side with our own: a world . . . from which the children could have escaped."

Could the green children be our strongest examples of a "parallel world connection?"

Friends of mine might have witnessed another instance of such a "connection." Jack Fox and his son, Craig, were hiking about ten years ago on the Appalachian Trail crossing Mount Guyot in the White Mountains of New Hampshire. It was a shivery, icy, rainy day. The two were wearily making their way, drenched to the soles of their hiking boots with water pouring from their faces and their packs, when suddenly a voice clear as a bell called to them. They paused and looked up, startled that anyone else was there.

Over on a boulder stood a man attired in a dark coat with a derby hat on and shining patent leather shoes! He was jauntily leaning on a silver-tipped cane with one outstretched hand.

"Please do be careful," he called out. "It's icing!"

Jack and his son nodded their appreciation and plodded on. But it was only a matter of seconds later that the two began to absorb what they had seen. Here in the cold of a mountain trail with sleet teeming around them, that man had been standing atop a rock, calm and *dry* as though he were in a rose garden!

The two began to reassess what had happened. They agreed the man, just as they were passing, had stepped down from his perch and coolly and easily crossed in front of them and disappeared over the rocks—in the direction of precipitous cliffs! What such a person dressed as he was and untouched as he seemed to be was doing there, the two could not imagine.

"I have always felt," says Craig today, "that he was a guardian angel. In all that mist we could have gone awry and off those cliffs if he hadn't stood there in that protecting sort of way—pressing us straight and safely ahead."

Where did the man in the dark coat and patent

leather shoes come from that day on the Appalachian Trail?

It is impossible to say but not impossible to conceive that he might have been from another Universe—an invisible one.

In a different vein, yet similar, too, there was the remarkable incident that occurred to Blaine Whittaker a few years ago. The young man was salmon fishing one evening off the coast of Washington state when he felt himself being overcome by escaping deadly engine fumes. He was just able to crawl to the deck before collapsing.

His thirty-two-foot boat, *Norma Jean*, roared out of control.

At that same time, a ham operator in the area picked up a distress signal. "Taking water. Losing power. The *Sylvia D.* Help!"

This SOS sent from near Point Roberts near the Canadian border was quickly relayed to the Coast Guard cutter *Britt*, operating out of Bellingham, Washington.

The cutter, skippered by Chief Petty Officer Kenneth Bird, chugged speedily northward. Pretty soon the radar screen showed a strange blip a few miles south of Point Roberts. It kept circling around and around. The captain thought the signal an odd one. The cutter kept going and shortly came upon the *Norma Jean* spinning out of control in circles. No one on board responded to their signals, so the Coast Guard boat pulled alongside. Two men boarded the boat, killed the throttle, and carried off the unconscious fisherman. It was Blaine Whittaker. Later, at the hospital in Richmond, British Columbia, Whittaker declared, "God was really looking over my shoulder!"

The story was a remarkable one. The *Britt* had continued its search that afternoon for the mysterious *Sylvia D.* with no success. Planes and other patrol boats had joined the search, but nothing was turned up.

In order to complete its records, the Coast Guard searched for the *Sylvia D.*'s registration, license, or documentation. They couldn't find one item. Concluded one Coastguardsman, "As far as we're concerned, the *Sylvia D.* never existed."

How could an SOS get sent from a ship that didn't exist?

From where, then, did the saving message come? That illusive invisible Universe?

So many questions face the wonder and curiosity of man. Enigmas such as the foregoing— and the following, to be found in the next chapter.

Chapter Ten

STRANGE FORCES

Bertrand Russell, English philosopher, writer, and mathematician once wrote, "Physics is mathematical not because we know so much about the physical world, but because we know so little: it is only its mathematical properties that we can discover."

What, then, are the *unknown* properties of our physical world that remain and challenge man's mind for discovery? Could the answer lie chiefly in the realm of universal forces? In the world of science four basic forces are known: the electromagnetic, the gravitational, and the weak nuclear and the strong nuclear forces. Is there a fifth force existent that has escaped man's detection, and if so, could it be the illusive "link" that ties us to a parallel Universe?

Many scientists today are keeping an open mind in regard to the possibility of a fifth type of energy. John White discussed this aspect in an article he authored for *Psychic* Magazine (February 1976).

"In recent years," wrote White, "an increasing number of investigators . . . have come to feel that science must recognize a new principle in nature— the same principle of vitality . . . that ancient traditions considered primary. . . ."

Then he goes on to report on what one researcher in this area has concluded: "There is an energy in living organisms that is weak and unpredictable, but it can be refracted, polarized, focused, and combined with other energies. It sometimes has effects similar to magnetism, electricity, heat, and luminous radiation, but it is none of these. Attempts to control and employ the energy have met with little success; investigators have not yet defined the laws governing its operation."

But careful consideration of all this may come up with a few possible instances in which certain rare people *have* been able to "employ the energy." People such as the remarkable ballet artists of this world over the years who have stunned audiences with an apparent ability to sustain their bodies in midair for lengths of time that defied gravitational law.

There was Maria Taglioni in the early and mid-

dle years of the 1800's. The daughter of a renowned Italian ballet master and composer of
ballets, young Maria, trained by her father, reached
the heights of fame. She was considered the greatest dancer of her day, capturing the hearts of
Paris audiences particularly when she appeared
there in 1832 in his ballet, *La Sylphide.* The critics
were ecstatic in their appraisal of her performance.
"She seems to be able to walk on a cornfield without bending the ears!" Other witnesses of her
technique claimed she could literally "stop in the
air!"

Then there was the renowned N. P. Damaschoff.
Nicolai Legat wrote admiringly of his talent. He
reported he saw the remarkable dancer not only
leap in an arc of beauty but stay "for some time in
the air."

But it is Vaslav Nijinsky, considered the greatest
dancer who ever lived, who demonstrated so superbly the uncanny ability to achieve elevation
and *sustain* it beyond any scientific plausibility.
In his biography of Nijinsky, the British author,
Cyril W. Beaumont, wrote:

"[Nijinsky's] elevation was really extraordinary.
That wonderful leap by which, as the sprite in
The Spectre de la Rose, he entered from the rose
garden, through the open French windows, to
alight beside the young girl asleep in her chair,
must still linger in the memories of all those who
saw it. There was a rose-coloured flash, and he
was seen to describe a graceful parabola with the
ease of a grasshopper leaping from one blade to

another. There was no flurry, no strained features, no thud as the feet came to the ground; it was just as though a rose petal had been caught up by a night breeze and wafted through the open window."

Later on the biographer describes the great Russian artist's exit in a ballet he witnessed when "it appeared as though the dancer had decided to fly, instead of walk off the stage; for as he made his exit, he suddenly rose in the air and disappeared behind the wings."

The mystery of the ability of these foregoing dancers to remain up in the air and descend slower than the law of gravitation would permit was a puzzle that challenged the widely known psychologist and analyst Nandor Fodor. He included a chapter in his book, *Between Two Worlds*, entitled "The Riddle of Vaslav Nijinsky."

His research into the background of the enigma proved one thing: Nijinsky himself did not know how he achieved momentary suspension. He knew only that he could and that it was natural and effortless.

Dr. Fodor talked with Nijinsky's widow, Romola, some years ago. She was herself a dancer and was well qualified to discuss her husband's unique prowess. She understood ballet supremely well and her husband even better. She told Dr. Fodor that when she once questioned Vaslav about his talent for suspension, he replied that he felt supported in the air. He knew that he could actually control the speed of his descent. He could come down as slowly or as rapidly as he wished.

Nandor Fodor was extremely interested in this process of control mentioned by Romola. He tells us, "To understand more about the riddle of Nijinsky's famous elevations we have to return to Hindu practices of generating a force that apparently counteracts gravitation. They say that he who awakens the *Anahata Chakra*, which is situated in the heart and is the seat of *Prana* (cosmic energy) 'can walk in the air.'"

A French anthropologist, Alexandra David-Neel, met such a mystic in Tibet at one time, Fodor relates. She declared, "The man did not run. He seemed to lift himself from the ground. . . ."

Did dancers like Taglioni, Damaschoff, and Nijinsky somehow, without their being aware of it, call upon and avail themselves of an anti-gravitation force that the average man is not aware exists? Does this force project itself from our parallel and invisible Universe? A rare clue to its presence which few men can recognize?

In addition to this remarkable buoying force there is evidence also of a strange energy that literally explodes in man's presence upon rare occasion, with no apparent source for it being detectable.

One of the first scientists to report on this phenomenon was Carl Jung, the noted psychologist. He was talking with his fellow scientist Sigmund Freud (actually arguing) upon the occasion of their meeting on March 25, 1909. The subject under discussion was precognition—the ability to see into the future.

Freud was firmly denying the possibility of such an ability when suddenly a loud report burst forth from a nearby bookcase. Both men stopped talking and turned in alarm.

Quickly Jung collected himself and explained, "That is an example of catalytic exteriorization phenomena!" To which Freud pronounced a clear "Bosh!"

Jung, however, smiled calmly and predicted that another explosion would shortly follow. Almost before he had finished his sentence, the second detonation occurred. Freud was so stunned by the incident that Jung didn't hear from him again for over three weeks.

This strange discharge of energy appears frequently also in reports of meetings with UFOs. Many witnesses have described hearing exploding sounds. Other contactees mention strange forces. A few years ago, a forty-one-year-old Wyoming oil-field worker claimed he was kidnapped by alien beings in a UFO while hunting in a remote wilderness region. He is Carl Higden of Rawlins, Wyoming.

Never one to involve himself in UFO lore, Carl was busy spending his wilderness days tracking down game. He drove his truck to the north edge of the Medicine Bow National Forest and got out. About four o'clock in the afternoon, rifle in hand, he came to a rise in the ground from where he spotted five elk grazing in a clearing a few hundred yards away. Delighted, he upped his rifle, lined up the largest buck in his telescopic sights, and pulled the trigger.

To his astonishment, instead of the usual blast and wrenching jolt, he watched the bullet float noiselessly out of the gun barrel *in slow motion!*

"It floated like a butterfly about fifty feet, and then fell to the ground," Carl later told a news reporter. Then came the shock of his life in the following moments. He heard a twig snap and turned to see a strange-looking man with "a head and face that seemed to extend directly into the shoulders, with no visible chin or neck."

Following that frightening encounter, Higden says he was taken aboard a spacecraft and not returned for hours later—a time when he was found back in his truck, radioing for help.

Strange story, indeed. Yet one undeniable result. The shell jacket of a 7mm bullet that was crushed when it smashed into *something*, invisible yet solid, was retrieved. Experts say that the odds against finding a spent bullet after it was fired are millions to one. Investigators into this Wyoming case suggested that the bullet was caught in a strange force field of some kind. Exactly what kind, no one is prepared to explain.

Yet, that doesn't mean to say such unknown forces as we have just described do not exist. No one has yet been able to say exactly what and where can be found our parallel Universe— or to say for sure that it does or does not exist. Yet that does not mean it doesn't exist. We can only be prepared to look and listen.

Many proponents of the invisible Universe theory feel we should start our searching in Egypt. In the next chapter we will take that look.

Chapter Eleven

PYRAMIDS AND TOMBS— SOURCES OF FORCES?

The mystery of a fifth force is one that has particularly intrigued Soviet scientists. Men like Leonid Vasiliev, physiologist at the University of Leningrad, have been working since the 1930's to establish proof of a new force's existence. They feel certain that a fifth force is a fact, though their experiments present them with the conclusion that nothing known to man so far can shield from this hypothesized force or contain it.

Did the ancients know how to contain it?

Of recent years many scientists the world over are asking that question. Did the Egyptians know how to "capture" a strange force or generate some kind of energy which present-day scientists have still not discovered? Can certain geometric forms such as a pyramid mobilize such a powerful force? Does shape affect matter?

The idea of shape having an influence on matter has received attention for some years now from the design engineers of many commercial companies in various countries. For example, a brewery in Czechoslovakia not so long ago decided to switch from the traditional round barrel for storage to angular-shaped barrels. The move was disastrous. The beer showed distinct signs of deterioration although the process of making the beer remained unchanged. The company had to revert to the old tried and true round barrel.

A French firm designed a new and special shape in which to package its yogurt because it found through experimentation that such a shape heightened and improved the microorganism action involved in the yogurt manufacturing process.

Making the leap, then, from manufacturers and designers of today to builders of the past, we come to those marvelous and puzzling monuments of ancient Egypt—the pyramids.

The significance of the pyramid structures has long been open to debate. The traditional concept is that the pyramids were religious monuments to the pharaohs, if not their actual tombs. But more recently, scientists like Dr. Kurt Mendelssohn, an emeritus professor fellow from Oxford University, feel that the true importance of the pyramids lay in the building of them, rather than in the use of the final product. This interesting analysis was presented recently by Dr. Mendelssohn to the American Association for the Advancement of Science (AAAS).

Technically, it would have been impossible for each pharaoh, upon ascending the throne, to order the building of a pyramid, argued Dr. Mendelssohn. He would have known it could not be completed in his lifetime. Also, explained the scientist, there were far more pyramids built than there were pharaohs to bury at that time.

The fact is, that as one pyramid work project tapered off, another one was commenced, declared Mendelssohn. This was because the pyramids were built as massive public works conceived of to advance the ancient Egyptian society economically as well as politically.

"It was the pyramid project rather than the pharaoh that was actually ruling Egypt," declared Mendelssohn. "And once its chief object, the creating of the state had been achieved, the project was allowed to run down without being resumed." He also pointed out that a parallel situation—a village economy replaced by a centralized state— existed in the valley of Mexico where two pyramids were built at Teotihuacan.

All of which may be the concluding argument to explain why there never has been found any trace of a burial of a pharaoh or his treasures in the Great Pyramid at Giza, that super-structure of them all.

The Great Pyramid of Pharaoh Khufu, called by

the Greeks "Cheops," was built over 4500 years ago at Giza in Egypt. It stands to this day as the most massive structure ever erected by man. To get an idea of its immensity, one can mull over the following staggering statistics: five cathedrals could be assembled within the thirteen-acre base. Its near two and a half million blocks of stone, weighing from two and a half tons to some fifty tons each, rise to a height of four hundred and eighty-one feet (the height of a forty-story skyscraper)! Napoleon contributed to these mind-boggling figures by estimating that the pyramid at Giza contained enough masonry to build a wall ten feet high and a yard wide around the whole of France!

The other dazzling aspects this structure presents arise from its astounding architectural know-how. So perfectly were the facing stones cut and fitted, for example, that a sheet of paper could scarcely be edged into the joints between! The southeast corner measures only a half-inch higher than the northwest corner. And the difference between the longest and shortest sides is less than eight inches—less than .09 percent!

Such remarkable accuracy in design and construction has led many researchers in pyramidology to assert that they could only have been built by superior intelligences from another Universe. Only the use of anti-matter devices unknown to our physics could have raised the weight and size of such blocks!

But more significant, perhaps, than the *outside*

miracles of the structures are those clues which lie hidden *within* relating to the effect of another Universe and its unique powers.

In his book, *Supernature*, Dr. Lyall Watson, biologist, archeologist, and anthropologist, discusses the fascinating possibility of the importance of the pyramid form. He details the following incident as an "extraordinary piece of evidence which suggests that shape could be important in receiving cosmic stimuli."

Some years ago, the Great Pyramid was visited by a Frenchman named Bovis, he tells us, "who took refuge from the midday sun in the pharaoh's chamber, which is situated in the center of the pyramid, exactly one-third of the way up from the base. He found it unusually humid there, but what really surprised him were the garbage cans that contained, among the usual tourist litter, the bodies of a cat and some small desert animals that had wandered into the pyramid and died there. Despite the humidity, none of them had decayed but just dried out like mummies. He began to wonder whether the pharaohs had really been so carefully embalming their subjects after all, or whether there was something about the pyramids themselves that preserved bodies in a mummified condition."

Watson goes on to report that Bovis returned home and made a scale model of the Cheops pyramid and placed it, like the original, with the base lines facing exactly north-south and east-west. Inside the model, exactly one third up, he placed a dead cat . . . then waited. True to his expectations, the dead creature mummified! The pyramid form, then, he concluded promotes dehydration!

News of this experiment reached a radio engineer in Prague, Czechoslovakia, named Karel Drbal. This scientist conducted the same experiment as that of Bovis and came up with the same results. Whereupon the Czech scientist concluded, "There is a relationship between the shape of a space inside the pyramid and the physical, chemical and biological processes going on inside that space."

Drbal recalled an old superstition that a razor left in the moonlight became blunted. He decided to try the possible reverse effect. Would a dull razor blade, for example, be sharpened by storage within the pyramid shape? He tried the experiment and found that, indeed, a dull blade became sharp again! Eventually, Drbal patented his discovery and manufactured what he called the "Cheops Pyramid Razor Blade Sharpener." A factory in Prague is still turning out miniature pyramids!

What happens inside the pyramid shape to cause such an effect?

Dr. Watson reasons that the edge of a razor blade has a crystal structure. Crystals, he tells us, are almost alive, in that they grow by reproducing themselves. When a blade becomes blunted, some of its edge crystals are rubbed off. Theoretically, Watson asserts, they should be able to replace themselves in time. So, possibly, "the Great Pyramid and its little imitations act as lenses that focus energy or as resonators that collect energy, which encourages crystal growth." Later Watson adds, "The pyramid shape itself is very much like that of a crystal magnetite, so perhaps it builds up a magnetic field."

Is the field the pyramid builds up not a magnetic one at all, but a fifth force, related to magnetism, but not identical with it, as John White (quoted earlier) told us?

A former NASA scientist, Nick Edwards of Encino, California, became interested in the Great Pyramid and its mysteries some ten years ago. He made a study of the strange properties he felt it contained within its stone walls. "The Great Pyramid is a very powerful source of life energy," Edwards told a reporter for the *National Insider* (February 1, 1976). "Recent research and my own experiments have shown that the shape of this pyramid when properly aligned to magnetic north acts as a resonator and accumulates 'biocosmic energy.'" Edwards maintains that this shape preserves fruit, milk, coffee, soft drinks, etc., in a state of freshness.

Agreeing with him is a physicist, Dr. Patrick Flanagan, who entered the Massachusetts Institute of Technology at the age of eleven and was once named in *Who's Who* as one of the top ten scientists in our country. Dr. Flanagan, like Nick Edwards, finds the pyramid a miraculous preserver of plants, and people as well. "People who place themselves under pyramids become mentally sharper and physically healthier," maintains Flanagan. Because the pyramid uses no fuel, costs nothing to maintain, and lasts indefinitely, Flanagan sees this shape as the ultimate answer to the energy crisis.

But more challenging to explanation than the preservative characteristic of the "captive force" of the pyramid is that which has been even more fascinating to man throughout the history of the ancient Egyptians: their apparent knowledge and application of a destructive force. In other words, if there is a fifth force mobilized by the pyramid shape? Can this power be generated for over thousands of years, strong enough to reach out and affect modern man? Were the ancient Egyptians aware of this and is this the energy left behind that is able to activate the ancient curses the Egyptians put upon their pyramidal monuments and their tombs—curses that strike down those who violate their sacred precincts?

One strong observation that has arisen from researchers' work into the Egyptian pyramids and the equally mystifying tombs of the kings is the fact that a prolonged stay inside by anyone seems to affect his mind. One of the earliest and most popularly related such experiences occurred, so goes the oft-repeated story, to none other than the dauntless Napoleon.

In 1798, after ringing victories in Italy, the great general turned his attention to indomitable England. He conceived of a military campaign that would outwit the shrewdest British military minds: he would attack England next—through Egypt; then would follow India! Ultimately, the whole world would be his!

In 1798 Napoleon and an army of 36,000 men set sail from Toulon in a fleet of 330 ships. The French met the forces of Mourad Bey, the governor for the Ottoman Turkish Empire, at Alexandria on the desert sands of Egypt. With a steady fury, the French rifles wrought their destruction on the fierce but inadequate fighting horsemen of the Turks. The Battle of the Pyramids was a matter of history in a few hours' time. Napoleon led his victorious column straight to the palace of Mourad Bey.

But the ambitious dictator had more on his mind than conquest of a near-legendary land. He wanted to delve into the mysterious monument of stone standing at Giza. On October 12th, the general made his visit to the Great Pyramid. He asked his aides to leave him. He wished to be alone in the king's chamber.

So much is history. What followed in subsequent moments remains obscure. Several accounts tell of it. One reported that the great leader came out noticeably upset. He refused to make any comment about his lone visit after he returned to quarters, but it is said that later when emperor of France, he told a friend he had seen a vision while standing next to the king's coffin. Just prior to his death on St. Helena, goes this story, he started to relate the experience to an aide, but then stopped short, as though thinking better of it.

When pressed to say more, the general merely shrugged his shoulders and walked off.

Another version that persists is the tale that after Napoleon visited the Great Pyramid, he returned to the palace and retired for the night. However, he was unable to sleep. He kept hearing a noise in the far corner of his bedchamber. He seized his sword, sat bolt upright, and called out. All he could see was an intense red light that fluttered and flared from the far corner of the room.

"Who are you?" demanded the astonished general.

The flame grew into the shape of a man.

"Who is Napoleon?" mocked the vision. "Your conquest of this land will not last! You have no more than a few years to make peace with the world!" With those words, the apparition disappeared.

The vision of a "Red Man" was seen by Napoleon for the remaining years of his life. That much has been mentioned by several of his contemporaries. As his death approached at St. Helena, it is said, the flaming man appeared for the final time as the dying commander pleaded for more time.

In a recent news bulletin published by the European Occult Research Society, a T. Aurandson wrote of the general's Egyptian experience:

"We know there are powerful energy patterns connected with the shape of the pyramid. Perhaps, Napoleon lingered for a time in the king's chamber. The energy in the pyramid may have created an electrical disturbance in his brain. This could have caused an altered state of consciousness that provided him with a perceptive glimpse of his own future."

Many years later, an English explorer by the name of Paul Brunton, as intrigued by the pyramids as was Napoleon, decided to have himself locked up for the night in the king's chamber in the Great Pyramid. After obtaining reluctant permission from the Cairo police chief, Brunton settled down in the deadly dark of the very room where Napoleon had stood. Brunton did not stand, however. He sat down in one corner of the room and waited, thoughtfully. Suddenly he found he could not think clearly any more. In his own words, written later of the event:

"Fear, fright and terror persistently showed me their terrible faces. Without my wanting them to, my hands were clasped together like a vise . . . My eyes were closed . . . always there was this unrelenting hostility—huge, elemental creations . . . grotesque shapes, madmen . . . and devilish apparitions passed around me. . . ."

By morning when Brunton was removed he was in a state of near total paralysis.

He was not the last person to be so affected. Many tourists in recent years have complained of being strangely influenced. In 1972 a Spanish lady was sent into a screaming frenzy at the upper end of the gallery. She could not move; her muscles contorted into cramps. Once she was outside, the cramps ceased.

H. V. Morton, who wrote a book called *Through the Lands of the Bible*, once wrote that he, too, experienced the horror of the Great Pyramid's strange forces. When in the king's chamber, he said he was suddenly overcome with a feeling of fear and panic. He ended up crawling out on all fours!

A well-known American archeologist, Professor George Reisner, made pyramid history in 1939 with the first radio broadcast ever to be conducted from inside the king's chamber. Yet three years later, in 1942, the scientist's strange death made as big news as had his famed broadcast. Reisner suddenly collapsed inside the pyramid and lay prone as if completely paralyzed. His associates quickly pulled him out into the open air and carried him to the camp quarters, where they tried desperately to revive him. Reisner died at the archeological camp site without ever regaining consciousness.

What goes on inside the mysterious pyramid at Giza? What affects man's mind? Is it an unknown energy contained therein that, at times, plays a destructive role in the form of a curse on man for violating sacred precincts?

Whatever it is, the pyramids of Egypt have not given us the answer yet. Scientists in 1968 who tried perhaps the most determinedly of all to come up with some kind of hard facts about the pyramids succeeded only in leaving us with the greatest puzzle of all. A team from the United States in collaboration with a group from Ein Shams University in Cairo together carried out a million-dollar project to x-ray the pyramid of Chephren, constructed just subsequent to that of Cheops.

The purpose was to discover possible hidden rooms in the pyramid. Accordingly they set up detectors in a chamber at its base which would measure the amount of cosmic-ray penetration, theorizing that more rays would pass through hollow areas in the six million tons of stone. The recorders ran daily for over a year. Finally, in early 1969 the latest computer (IBM 1130) arrived at the university for analysis. The results were unbelievable. The scientists had to admit defeat. The pyramid's cosmic-ray action made no sense at all! Tapes recorded at the same spot on successive days came up with completely different cosmic-ray patterns!

The guiding hand of the project, the Egyptian scientist, Amr Gohed, declared to reporters later, "This is scientifically impossible! Call it what you will—occultism, the curse of the pharaohs, sorcery or magic, there is some force that defies the laws of science at work in the pyramid!"

Is this defiant force related more to "curse power" than to the influence of a particular shape? Some investigators into Egyptian mysteries maintain that it is, since strange effects emanate as much, if not more, from the Egyptian tombs in the famed Valley of the Kings and at Sakkara (Memphis's City of the Dead) as from the pyramids. The substance and background of the pharaohs' curses seem to be of more significance than the shape of the place that housed them, feel many psychology investigators into the mystery.

The Egyptians had an obsession with the other world and the requirements for getting safely into it. The famous Cult of the Dead, which originated in India, reached its culmination in Egypt. In the early dynasties, the Egyptians believed that only royalty was admissible to the realm of eternal life. Gradually, the belief admitted nobles and high officials and, eventually, all "good men" were acknowledged as able to enter the gates of immortality.

The chief god of ancient Egypt was Osiris. He ruled in the regions of the dead. It was he who fathered all the pharaohs of the land. So preoccupied with death was the ancient race in this country that they allotted the length of the fruitful valley of the Nile to serve as the burial place for the dead.

These people believed that a man's soul could only enter the blessed realm of Osiris *if his body remained intact* in the place where he had lived on earth. This led to tremendous importance being put upon the preservation of the body and an unviolated tomb. The worst act of desecration that could be committed, according to the ancient Egyptians, was to despoil a tomb and/or remove a mummy from its coffin.

Consequently, the funeral service was a most solemn and fear-instilling ceremony. Terrible curses were threatened on any despoilers. To be certain of effect, these curses were inscribed on the walls of the death chambers because of the intense belief the Egyptians had in the magic of the written word. They believed that the very act of writing out a curse on a wall, a plaque, or a vase, or whatever, would ensure its effectiveness throughout all time.

Can there be such a thing as a thought force that spans fifty centuries of time?

A few years ago, the editor of the German *Playboy* magazine, Philipp Vandenberg, became so fascinated with such a possibility that he decided to research it in depth and then write a book about it, which he did (The English translation was published by Lippincott in 1975). He called it *The Curse of the Pharaohs*.

One of the first things Vandenberg's investigation brought to light was the fact that archeologists, a professional group as a whole, had strong reactions to the tomb-curse fear. Some dismissed the curse as plain nonsense; others refused to even talk about it, much less consider entering a pharaoh's tomb. As one Munich scientist put it when asked what he would fear, he replied, "The gods."

Vandenberg found that an unusually high number of archeologists in Egypt had died mysteriously. He tells, for one example, of Walter Bryan Emery, an Englishman who headed a digging operation in the cemetery at Sakkara, south of Cairo —an area referred to as Memphis's City of the Dead. As he stood over a shaft in March of 1971, Emery held a small statuette in his hand, an image of the ancient Death God, Osiris. He studied the tiny image from every angle. Later he walked with his assistant back to the office in Sakkara. The aide, weary from the heat, stretched out on a couch. Emery walked into the washroom.

In a few minutes the assistant heard moaning. He looked up and asked, "Are you sick?" He saw Emery leaning on the washbasin. He did not reply. He stood there as if paralyzed. The assistant grabbed him and pulled him to the couch. He called an ambulance and rushed the professor to the hospital in Cairo. The diagnosis reported the scientist was paralyzed on the left side. He never spoke again. He died the next day.

Other scientists Vandenberg checked out had suffered strange maladies. One suffered delirium after work in Egypt excavations. Another lost weight and couldn't think coherently any more. Still another, the great French archeologist Francois Champollion (who deciphered the Rosetta Stone) died with a paralytic disorder after returning from Egypt. He was only forty-two years old.

In summing up his research, the author declared, "It seemed as if the curse of the pharaohs exercised some magic force on its victims. Outstanding scholars were committing suicide for the sake of science or at least they were returning from Egypt somewhat mad."

No greater so-called "curse power" ever made itself felt, however, than that which appears to have made a dazzling and disturbing effect when the tomb of King Tutankhamen was discovered

over half a century ago. The results of that archeological find have puzzled and astounded researchers through all the years since.

King Tut, as he came to be called in America
after the discovery of his tomb, was a relatively
minor figure in Egyptian history. He was a mere
youth sitting on the throne as a puppet controlled
by a powerful cabal of priests. The young man
reigned only nine years, from 1358 to 1349 B.C.
But his name skyrocketed to importance thousands of years later when two hard-seeking British
archeologists unearthed his tomb in 1923 in the
fabled Valley of the Kings. They were Howard
Carter and Lord Carnarvon.

Lord Carnarvon was a devil-may-care explorer
and adventurer who had a passion for archeological searching in Egypt. Teamed with him on this
goal was an oldtime, experienced British archeologist, Howard Carter. The two men started the
project of pharaoh-tomb hunting in the Valley just
before World War I. At the end of the war, they
started afresh, convinced that the tomb of Tutankhamen lay somewhere in the already well-dug up
Valley of the Kings probably hidden under the
debris stashed around from earlier diggings. They
were so right. Late in 1922 the remains of some
workmen's huts were found—always indicators
that a royal tomb is nearby.

Carnarvon was in England. Carter loyally de-
nied himself the pleasure of further digging up the
actual tomb until his patron could arrive. Lord
Carnarvon was on the spot in a few weeks' time.

When the diggers finally uncovered a flight of steps and then a door sealed with the seal of Tutankhamen, one of the most exciting times in archeological history was born.

The actual tomb unearthing and entering took place the following February. Twenty Egyptologists assembled for the big moment. It was a breathtaking one. The scope of the gold, silver, ivory, and precious stones was beyond conception. Then came the sarcophagus itself, which opened to reveal inner coffins with a pure gold effigy of Tutankhamen. From the third was drawn the mummified body of the young man with his face and head remarkably preserved.

The moment was a glory felt around the world that February of 1923. Newspapers carried the news of the discovery to every corner of the earth. Fashions and jewelry designs quickly became Egyptian-oriented. King Tut and Howard Carter and Lord Carnarvon along with the royal personage became the men of the hour.

But scholars and diggers at the site were far less elated. They spoke uneasily to interviewers and investigators at the spot. There was one item that had been completely—and quite deliberately overlooked by the enthusiasts. It was a clay tablet that Carter had found in the tomb's antechamber. It bore an ominous message:

Death will slay with his wings
Whoever disturbs the peace of the pharaoh

Carter shrugged his shoulders when the translation was presented to him. It didn't bother him or the transcriber, nor some of the scholars at his side at that moment. But Carter was uneasy about the effect it might have on his Egyptian laborers. He had the clay tablet removed from the list of items catalogued within the tomb. Even the tablet itself became lost. No one knows where it is to this day.

Later, another curse was uncovered. It was written on the back of a statue found in the main chamber of the tomb. It read:

It is I who drive back the robbers of the tomb with the flames of the desert.

I am the protector of Tutankhamen's grave.

This item, too, was quickly removed from sight and knowledge of the Egyptian helpers. Then a third item was found—an alabaster vase bearing the same inscription as on the clay tablet. Lord Carnarvon, it is said, picked up the vase, putting his fingers inside. When he withdrew his hand, there was a drop of blood on his fingertip, an experience said to have made His Lordship uneasy.

Discovery of the fabulous tomb was just the beginning of the work to be done. For one thing, complicated arrangements had to be made to raise and remove the mummy of King Tut. Lord

Carnarvon, elated with the success of his project, motored back to Cairo, where he had engaged a suite at the Hotel Continental. Carter lodged at Luxor.

It was only six weeks after the opening of the tomb that Carter got word that Lord Carnarvon was gravely ill with a high fever. When he arrived at the Cairo hotel, Carnarvon was unconscious. His wife, Lady Almina, sat at his side. At two in the morning, the English nobleman died. The world was shocked. What had happened? At first, the doctors declared he had cut himself while shaving, opening an old wound that became infected. Then the diagnosis was changed to the poisonous aftereffects of a mosquito bite. Actually, it was never finally determined what caused his death.

But the sudden passing of the leader of the expedition caused a whisper across the world: had a curse of the ancient tomb been stirred?

A few weeks later, American archeologist Arthur Mace who had helped Carter clear the entry to the main chamber of the tomb suddenly complained of feeling exhausted. He lay down to rest and fell into a deep coma. He died in the same Continental Hotel in Cairo as had Lord Carnarvon.

On the heels of this tragic end, an old friend of Carnarvon's, George Jay Gould, son of the famous American industrialist, hurried to Egypt. Carter took him out to the excavation. The next day, Gould fell ill with a high fever, and he died that night.

Within five months, Lord Carnarvon's half-brother, Aubrey Herbert, M.P., who had visited the tomb, died. On the heels of that, a South African millionaire, Woolf Joel, who had been yachting on the Nile, fell down a flight of stairs and died from a stroke. Arthur Weigall, Inspector of Egyptian Antiquities at the time of the tomb opening, died of what was diagnosed as "an unknown fever."

The following year of 1924 the curse seemed to pursue its victims unrelentingly. Several Egyptians fell to sudden ends. Prince Ali Fahmy was shot to death in the fashionable Savoy Hotel in London while his brother, Hallah Bey, committed suicide. Both men claimed descent from the pharaohs. Fahmy had been present at the opening of the Tut tomb. So was the Sirdar of the Egyptian Army, Sir Lee Stack Sirdah. He was assassinated that same year.

Archibald Douglas-Reid was the radiologist specially selected to unbind the mummy of the king and x-ray the body. Shortly afterwards, the scientist complained of feeling weary and feeble. He returned to England and died there shortly afterwards.

At the same time the radiologist was summoned, Carter sent for a well-known photographer, Frank Raleigh, to come to Egypt to photograph the Tut sarcophagus. He did so and within a short time complained of weakening eyesight. He soon went completely blind and died shortly afterwards.

In the same year of 1924, two scientists involved with the entry of the Tut tomb, Professor Laffleur of McGill University in Canada and a young Egyptologist, H. E. Evelyn-White, died suddenly, the latter by his own hand. He left a note stating: "I knew there was a curse on me!"

The death of these two men was followed by that of a signmaker at the British Museum who had made identification labels for many of the treasures and relics from the tomb.

Two years later the grisly list was still growing. Two French archeologists who were present at the tomb's opening died suddenly. They were Dr. Pasanova and Dr. Georges Benedite.

The year 1929 saw more additions. Lord Carnarvon's stepmother died of a mysterious insect bite. Carnarvon's secretary and assistant, the Hon. Richard Bethel, died in London of a circulatory collapse. His home had for years served as a storage center for many of the Tut treasures. A few months later, Bethel's father, Lord Westbury, threw himself from the seventh floor of his London flat. Adding to the weirdness of the case, the alabaster vase brought from the tomb by his son (which bore the curse inscription quoted earlier) was found in Lord Westbury's bedroom. Following this series of tragedies occurred the strangest of all. As the Lord's funeral procession proceeded toward Golders Green, the hearse ran over and killed an eight-year-old child by the name of Joseph Greer of Battersea.

Within a few years Mrs. Bethel was dead, and during the early years of World War II, Lady

Westbury was bombed out of her home in Putney.

Before 1929 was through, seven more scientists connected with the excavation of the Tutankhamen tomb were dead. Professors Winlock and Foucrat and archeologists Harkness and Davies. Also the two men who performed an autopsy on Tut's body died, chemist Alfred Lucas and Dr. Derry. Carter's two assistants, Astor and Callender, passed on suddenly. It had been Callender who had translated the curse inscriptions for the expedition.

In 1935 Professor James Breasted of the University of Chicago, who had been actively engaged in the uncovering of the tomb, died of a severe streptococcal infection. That same year felled the last of the Tut victims, an American writer, Louis K. Siggins, who had authored a play about the mysterious deaths related to the Tut curse!

Over thirty people connected with the discovery of the tomb of King Tutankhamen died strangely.

"Death will slay with his wings whoever disturbs the peace of the pharaoh."

The Egyptian curse power, so called, would seem to have existed in relation to other "disturbed" ancient mummies in addition to Tut. There is the story of the lost hand of the Princess who was the sister-in-law of Tutankhamen. Being a daughter of the Pharaoh Akhnaton and a rebel against his newly instituted religious doctrines, she suffered rape, torture, and death at the command of her father, so the story goes. The final insult was the cutting off of her right hand by the priests. It was then buried secretly in the Valley of the Kings. Being without her whole, intact body, the young woman would be forbidden entry into immortality. But quite conversely, the lurid incident has made her immortal.

It seems the mummified right hand was found and kept by a local sheik in Luxor who eventually gave it as a gift to Count Louis Hamon and his wife, who returned to England with it. It was not long afterwards in that year of 1922 when Hamon awakened one night to see the form of an Egyptian female standing in the doorway. In the next moment she vanished. Later, Hamon discovered the mummified hand was gone. Two days later, the count read in the papers of the discovery of the tomb of Tutankhamen.

Feeling somehow there was a weird connection or a warning of some kind, Hamon wrote Lord Carnarvon immediately of his experience with the vanished hand. "The ancient Egyptians possessed knowledge and powers of which we today have no comprehension," wrote the count. "Take care not to offend their spirits."

Carnarvon was impressed. He thought twice about entering the tomb. But Carter had no ear for such nonsense and burrowed full speed ahead. The possible consequences of the act we have just reviewed.

But another even more fascinating Egyptian curse story had commenced its course a few years before the Tut case. This relates to the mummy case of another princess of ancient Egypt who had been a high priestess in the Temple of Amon-Ra in Thebes. She enjoyed tremendous popularity during the reign of Amenhotep IV (the heretic pharaoh who changed his name to Ikhnaton). Her grave was found in Tell el-Amarna. She had served in a temple called by the arresting name of "Temple of the Eyes."

A close examination of her mummy case made her temple associations very clear. Its outside bore her image worked in gold and enamel, but it was the wonder of the eyes that caught the attention of all who looked upon her gold-wrought features. The almond-shaped eyes seemed to "come alive," people exclaimed, and their shining malevolence was so direct and powerful those who gazed into them said they made their "blood turn to ice" with their evil look.

In the mummy case were several artifacts, though the body itself had long since been missing. One object was an amulet in the figure of the Death God, Osiris. It bore a tiny inscription:

. . . "a glance of your eyes will triumph over everything that is done against you."

The small image had lain beneath her head. Was it a prophecy?

An Englishman named Douglas Murray spent a good many years of his life in Egypt toward the end of the last century. He was fascinated by its ancient lore. He was offered the mummy case of the ancient princess, and he readily bought it as a special object of interest. He knew nothing of the curse at that time, but he was delighted with his purchase and had it packed up and sent to London. A few days after the purchase, Murray was on a shooting trip up the Nile when unaccountably the gun in his hand exploded. In great pain he was rowed back to Cairo. But the headwinds were of unusual force, and the trip was so delayed that by the time he was placed in the hospital at Cairo, gangrene had set in and his arm had to be amputated.

Tragedy struck his companions also. Two of them fell suddenly ill on the voyage back to England and died at sea. Two Egyptian laborers who had carried the case died within that year. When the ship bearing Murray docked in England, it was found many of the treasures he had acquired had been stolen.

Shortly after his arrival, a friend of his became interested in the mummy case. She was a well-known writer and an avid fan of all things mysterious. Murray gave her the case, gladly. Upon her arrival home, her mother hurried down the stairs to meet her, slipped, and broke her thigh bone. From this incident, she soon became gravely ill, and she was dead in a short time.

Then the four dogs of the writer became ill with nothing any veterinarian could diagnose. All four dogs died. At this same time, the woman's fiancé parted company with her, giving no explanation whatsoever. Following that, the writer herself became desperately ill—so ill, in fact, she sent for her lawyer and instructed him to draw up her will.

The lawyer, after hearing the story, firmly advised her to return the mummy case to Douglas Murray. She did so and almost immediately recovered and felt in fine health.

Murray, however, was still too ill from his traumatic experience to cope with the relic. He felt its ownership was a risk for any particular person, and he decided to put it up for sale to an organization or art group—an impersonal ownership that would surely be beyond any direct vendetta of an ancient Egyptian priestess and her curse.

In preparation for this proposed sale, Murray called on a photographic studio on Baker Street to take a picture of it which he could include in a prospectus. He had the case taken down to the studio as soon as he could arrange it.

Within a week he received word from the photographer: the picture had come out showing a *living* face with staring, gleaming eyes! Before Murray could obtain a copy, the photographer suddenly died! And from no apparent physical cause!

This was all too much. Murray gave up all ideas of selling the object and determined he would dispose of it by presenting it to a large institution that couldn't possibly be affected by a personal demoniacal object. The British Museum was surely above any kind of target position. He would give the case to them.

Too ill to make the formal arrangements himself, Dougles Murray enlisted the aid of an old friend, an Egyptologist, who willingly agreed to help. This man, while awaiting the decision of the Council of the British Museum to approve the donation, asked permission to keep the case in his own house. It would provide him with comfortable time in which to study the hieroglyphics on the case. Accordingly, he had the Egyptian treasure removed to his own home. Murray was shocked to hear, within a few weeks time, that his friend had been found dead in bed, an empty bottle of chloral (a narcotic) found on his bedside table. The man's unfortunate end was called by the examiner "death by misadventure." At the inquest, the valet testified that from the day the mummy case had come into the house, his master had suffered from insomnia and had resorted to taking the drug in order to get to sleep.

Shortly thereafter, the British Museum accepted the mummy case, the trustees proclaiming it one of the most perfect of its kind and an excellent example of coffin decoration under the XVIIIth Dynasty.

Almost at once, troubles ensued. The carrier who did the transporting was dead within a week, while of the two porters who carried it up the museum steps, one fell on the stairway and broke his leg; the other died suddenly the next day, though in good health.

But laying all this to coincidence, the museum proudly place the case on exhibit in its Egyptian

161

wing. But again, strange things began to happen. A well-known artist who drew the fascinating object was run over by a horse and cab as he left the museum. The sketch he was carrying of the case was completely destroyed.

Another visitor to the wing who declared the case's high priestess looked like "an ugly old hag" fell from his bicycle on his way home and broke an arm. A lady who passed by the case and pronounced it a hideous relic accidentally set herself on fire that same evening and was badly disfigured. A photographer who was granted permission to film the case in the museum afterwards fell down and broke his nose.

Shortly after these incidents, Dr. E. A. Wallis Budge, the director of Egyptian antiquities at the museum, was approached by a press photographer who asked permission to photograph the now famous exhibit at the museum and run a story on it in one of London's newspapers. Still unable to accept the series of incidents as anything more than weird coincidence, Dr. Budge agreed.

The next day the photographer returned in high excitement and showed the director a print. "Look, sir, the face on the case is of a *living* woman!" There, again, were the luminous, staring eyes of a human female face. Dr. Budge could scarcely believe what he was looking at. After leaving the museum, the photographer went straight home and for no known accountable reason, locked the door to his bedroom and shot himself.

Dr. Budge and the rest of the museum staff now

began to see that what had been considered "entertaining superstition" attached to the "demon mummy case" was now a serious threat. No less than thirteen people connected with that ancient relic since it had been donated were now dead. The museum staff decided to remove the case from public exhibition. They would relegate it to the vaults below.

That decision brought its problems. No one wanted to be an agent involved in the moving. Finally two attendants reluctantly agreed to transport the case, if the chief messenger of that wing would oversee the move. Accordingly the latter agreed and took charge. After the move was completed, one of the attendants sprained his ankle as he hurried back up the stairs. A few days later, the chief messenger was found dead at his desk.

From that time on, however, all was at peace at the British Museum in its Egyptian wing. The high priestess lay quietly at rest away from mankind's vision in the storage vaults beneath.

About this time, rumors told of a bizarre ending to the mummy case. A Lord Canterville, on behalf of the British Museum, so goes the story, agreed to handle a disposition of the troublesome treasure. He sold it to the Metropolitan Museum in New York City. Accordingly, Canterville had the mummy case carefully packed in a wooden crate and made arrangements for it to be transported to America by the surest, fastest, and safest means possible. He chose the maiden voyage of the

White Star Line's newest ship, the fastest, safest vessel afloat—the *Titanic*.

He personally spoke to the ship's commander, Captain Edward J. Smith, who assured him the mummy case would receive his personal attention. It would not be stored in the hold of the ship, but behind the command bridge. Of course, the ship, which pulled out of Southampton in April of 1912, never made port. She struck an iceberg off Newfoundland on the night of April 14th and sank with a loss of over eighteen hundred lives.

This story has received wide acceptance over the years since the *Titanic* disaster. Even the scholarly and thorough researcher, Philipp Vandenberg (like many writers before him) thought the evidence he uncovered pointed to the truth of the tale. In his book, *The Curse of the Pharaohs*, he discusses the puzzling behavior of the *Titanic*'s captain that night, noting that Captain Smith, in spite of years of experience at sea, permitted a poor course for the vessel at an excessive speed and failed to alert the passengers to any danger even though he, himself, at the sudden drop of temperature (from 43°F at seven in the evening to freezing point by ten) should have realized impending danger from floating ice in the vicinity.

Vandenberg brings up the provocative thought: Could Captain Smith, too, have looked into those fatal radiant eyes of the mummy-case? Was he, too, a victim of the curse?

To consider the possibility of such an event, I recently traveled to England to check on the possible present whereabouts of the mummy case. Could it still be in existence?

It could, and it is.

It stands serenely and without pretension in the Egyptian Wing of the British Museum in London.

But this fact, I learned, does not preclude the possibility that the Captain Smith incident could be true. The mummy case, I was told by an old guard at the museum, *was* on the *Titanic*. After the tragedy it was found floating in the water and was picked up and returned to the British Museum.

The authorities at that venerable institution today smile at the story. "We have moved the case out of the wing in the past and stored it below at one time, but it never left the museum."

An old-time guard snorted at this declaration. "If the mummy case of Amon-Ra didn't leave the museum, it sure wanted to! Why, I can remember when every morning it was found to have moved. They finally had to nail it in place to keep it still!"

One member of the staff kept a log of various disturbances years ago. He noted they were minor in nature, and soon occurred less frequently, until nothing happened at all. The case of the "demon mummy case" was eventually lost to public attention, where it still lies, peacefully unobtrusive and innocent.

But Vandenberg's point of possible affliction from "radiant eyes" of the Amon-Ra mummy case is still a logical question to consider in the light of his in-depth research to ascertain what could have made old Egyptian tomb and coffin curses so apparently effective. The possible answers he came up with are most interesting and worthy of review.

For one thing, he found that in the list of victims the cause of death related to one of three basic fatal illnesses almost entirely: fever with delusions, strokes accompanied by circulatory collapse, or sudden terminal cancers.

From this significance he proceeded to uncover what kinds of causes occasion such dire physical responses. His research was revelatory.

Poisons were one of the ancient Egyptian "specialities." They had extensive knowledge of them; their priests and doctors made skillful use of them and their "magic powers." As the Parisian toxicologist, Dr. M. Martiny, states, the drying up of poisons does not decrease their potency. Although ultraviolet rays can neutralize poisons, such rays cannot penetrate tombs of stone such as the pharaohs'. Pyramids and cliff rock would have made excellent storing places for poisons.

This possibility reaches high acceptance in the case of the afflicted scientists when one considers, Vandenberg points out, that taking it in small doses, man could become immune. Howard Carter, who spent half his life shut up in various Egyptian tombs, could have built up a resistance. He did, however, complain frequently of paralyzing attacks of dizziness and weariness, hallucinations and headaches, all symptoms of poisoning.

The effects of bacteria are also an additional source of trouble to consider, Vandenberg states.

Although the ancient Egyptians didn't know bacteria by name, they understood their physiological effects and treated them with natural drugs. Most bacteria are nourished by vegetable and animal substances, and of course, mummies were heavily treated with fats, oils, and resins. Can bacteria survive centuries and cause biochemical infections? Chemists say that such could be the case with some types.

Were the reports of paralysis, delirium, weakness, disrupted consciousness, circulatory difficulties, etc., relating to the tomb "curse" victims so predominantly due to these factors brought forward by Vandenberg? The plausibility is strong.

The final hypothesis put forth by the German editor is possibly the most cogent and the most interesting. Radiation.

Author Vandenberg explores many case histories of death due to exposure to radiation. The similarities in effects of these to those experienced by the tomb victims are striking. In 1949, this researcher tells us, the atomic scientist, Professor Luis Bulgarini, astonished archeologists by declaring that he believed the ancient Egyptians understood the laws of atomic decay. Their priests and wise men were familiar with uranium. Bulgarini felt it was definitely possible that they used radiation in order to protect their holy places. Even to this day, rock with uranium content is mined in Egypt, the author explains. Further, reaction to radiation is varied. Some are deeply affected, others not at all. The results of the

Hiroshima bomb prove that: many died; a few survived, scarcely affected at all. All of which could explain why so many related to the tombs' entries died while a few were unaffected, such as the indomitable Howard Carter, who lived until 1939.

In his conclusion, Vandenberg brings us back to the concept of "other world forces." Why did the ancient Egyptians, asked the author, build their cemeteries so far from human habitation? The City of the Dead of Thebes was in the Valley of the Kings; Memphis built its grave field at Sakkara and the pyramids at Giza. Was it because these regions were "special"? Were they "windows" to out-of-this-world influences and forces about which we know nothing but to which the ancient Egyptians were keenly alert? These people, Vandenberg feels, were on the trail of phenomena which we are only beginning to consider seriously."

So we are left with many rousing thoughts about the ancient curse of the Egyptian tombs—many possible explanations to consider. One thing seems sure: the answer is far less mystical and mysterious than had earlier been supposed as scientists begin analyzing the many factors. Certainly, the key to handling the puzzle is in man's own consciousness more than anywhere else. Thoughts and analysis bring enlightenment; fear and superstition do the greatest harm—more than poisons, bacteria, and radiation, when you come right down to it.

The renowned psychologist, analyst, and writer, Nandor Fodor, researched extensively into the Egyptian curse and its apparent powers. He called a curse "a malignant suggestion." What a comforting analysis! *Suggestion*, not fact. We never need accept a *suggestion*. How reassuring that thought is—no matter how malignant the suggestion, we can always dispose of it by refusing to listen to it, be persuaded by it, or be influenced by it! How useless that response renders the most malignant suggestion ever thought up or written out!

In conclusion, after all that's been said, done, or thought about in relation to the dire tomb curses of the Egyptians, perhaps writer-researcher Frank Usher put it the best and simplest of all in his piece, "Ghosts of Ancient Egypt": "It has been observed that people who believe in curses are more likely to be struck down by them." And I add that psychology today reveals how easily one can accept beliefs without knowing it, unconsciously, either one's own or a collective belief in the thought of mankind.

So we are left with the last and most vital clue that lies only as far away as your next thought. When it comes to searching for an alternate Universe, need we look any further than man's own mind for the key?

Chapter Twelve

THE UNSEEN UNIVERSE OF CONSCIOUSNESS

In the foregoing chapters we have done a lot of looking at the possibility of an invisible twin Universe, another whole like us, yet different. Proponents call it various terms such as Invisible Universe, Antimatter Universe, Parallel Universe, Fourth Dimension . . . but they all attribute the same characteristics to this unknown unit. It is unmaterial, therefore unseeable by man's eyes or his instruments. It interacts with or interpenetrates our physical universe from time to time, an action known only by reaction. Phenomena inexplicable in scientific terms are occurring, and in these instances, perhaps, we are being notified of the Invisible System's proximity to us.

There is another analysis that we have not discussed in detail. Is this unseen Universe purely a mental state? Are UFO's, Pyramidology, Atmospheric Influences and Geographic Influences, Dematerialization, etc., all "psychic" construents?

Is the fourth dimension or the great Invisible Universe not a place—either physical or unphysical—but a state of mind? A product of a mortal man's own beliefs about himself and his Universe? An emanation from a subtle repository of material man's thoughts—a universal and collective storehouse of suggestions and traditional concepts from which the world's mass mind unconsciously draws and then objectifies?

A typical product of such processing can be seen in the UFO phenomenon. Examined in the light of this "mass mind" one sees a correlation between what is objectified and what is objectifying.

Jacques Vallée, the noted French astrophysicist and UFO investigator, makes this point time and time again: Man has, since the beginning of his days on earth, witnessed unidentified flying objects. UFO's, Vallée asserts, have been seen throughout history and have consistently provided their own explanation within the framework of each culture. In antiquity they were regarded as gods; in medieval times, as magicians; in the nineteenth century, as scientific geniuses. And, finally, in our own time, as interplanetary travelers.

Objectifications from a mortal mass mind?

Author and phenomena-investigator John A. Keel would support this theory as he has stated on numerous occasions that he concludes that all paranormal manifestations stem from a common source, no matter what frame of reference they occur within. This common source probably is not a tangible, structured technology but a process of thought power. The phenomenon of UFO's illustrates that this power is able to manipulate the human mind and reality itself to conform to—and support—the beliefs of the witnesses.

Wasn't Dr. Hynek (see Chapter Two) suggesting the same thing when he asked, "[Are UFO's] a product of our own minds without our being aware of it?" John White, an editor with *Psychic* magazine, expounds in an article in the February 1976 issue thoughts that arouse and challenge. He contends that "These questions bring us slowly but surely to the realization that only by understanding the essence of ourselves—the layers of the psyche, including our higher Self and our highest Self—can we understand the nature and structure of the cosmos." And I would add: "and any and all other universes that may exist."

"Where are these higher planes, these hyperspaces, these other dimensions?" asks White in his summation paragraph. "All sources agree: they are within us, even though they seem to be outside us in physical space; and at the same time, they are indeed *out there....*"

Can these higher dimensions of thought *within* us affect the physical space outside us?

There is mounting evidence that man has the ability through rising concepts in consciousness to overcome physical space dictates even to the extent of bettering his life on earth and his physical environment as well. When man cleans up the atmosphere of his mind, many philosophers feel, the Universe will reflect this purified subjective state in clearer skies, fewer storms, tornadoes, earthquakes, and extremes of heat and cold. With such exalted reasoning we can come to a beautiful conclusion that would have pleased Mark Twain no end. Man, at long last, is not only talking about the weather, he finds he can do something about it!

The late Oliver Reiser, a philosopher of note, took that theory one step further. There is a kind of exalted transference of thought going on in the Great Whole, he contended. A Supreme Consciousness, that is the highest Mind possible which reaches down to humanity—to which humanity in turn reaches up and thus is established the most infinitely, mentally pure Universe possible. And that would be the only true universe there is. Others could only hint at its perfection.

And so the probe for a greater understanding of our surroundings goes on. In the *Christian Science Monitor* of June 18, 1975, Robert C. Cowen wrote a piece concerning man's search for life beyond us. He stated:

"There is more than scientific curiosity behind this effort. Many interested scientists believe that mankind faces such awesome problems that it will either destroy itself or find a creative solution that will amount to the rebirth of civilization. They think that all technological civilizations probably face such a challenge at about our stage of development. If other worlds are sending messages, they reason, these civilizations probably have surmounted this challenge and we might learn from their experience."

Then Cowen concludes his article with the following statement:

"The greatest outreach the human race has yet made, an attempt to contact other worlds, is motivated partly by a yearning to transcend the problems of 20th-century earth."

In this ultimate transcendence, then, can it not be agreed, man will take his first step out of this world into that other unphysical Universe, wherever it is?

THE BEST OF BESTSELLERS
FROM WARNER BOOKS!